SURVIVING THE BLUES gives voice to the concerns of women whose adult lives have been framed by the dramatic and cumulative changes wrought by the Thatcher government in a decade of uninterrupted rule. The stories collected here are an inspiring testimony to the courage, humour and resilience of this younger generation of feminists, and the oppositional values that have sustained them during this period.

JOAN SCANLON teaches twentieth-century literature and drama and coordinates the degree course at London Contemporary Dance School. She also teaches for the Open University course on The Changing Experience of Women, and is writing a book on censorship, sexuality and the modern novel for Polity Press. She lives in London.

Best wishes

& Thanks for coming

out on a Monday night

Joan Scanlon

SURVIVING THE BLUES

GROWING UP IN THE THATCHER DECADE

EDITED BY
JOAN
SCANLON

VIRAGO

Published by VIRAGO PRESS Limited 1990
20–23 Mandela Street, Camden Town, London NW1 0HQ
This collection and introduction copyright © Joan Scanlon 1990
Copyright © in each contribution held by the author 1990

A CIP catalogue record for this book is available from the
British Library

Typeset by CentraCet, Cambridge
Printed in Great Britain by
Cox & Wyman Ltd, Reading, Berkshire

For Cassie, Eleanor and Jennie
and girls growing up in the '90s

CONTENTS

Preface and Acknowledgements

From the beginning this book has been a close collaboration with my editor at Virago and friend of many years, Lucinda Montefiore. We have shared a very particular commitment to this project and felt equally challenged by it, having grown into feminism since the beginning of the eighties when we met in our early twenties, and finding ourselves in that middle ground between our older sisters who were active in the Women's Liberation Movement of the seventies and the women who write in this book. We have discussed the issues raised here with a number of other women during the last year, and I would like to thank all those who have listened, advised, enthused and supported us. For myself, I am especially grateful to Su Kappeler who has inspired and encouraged me, and been my most rigorous critic. Amongst those who have suggested contributors, or who have supported any of us in writing this book, I would particularly like to thank Kum Kum Bhavnani, Kath Gordon, Liz Kelly, Annette McAllister, Nell McCafferty, Jean McCrindle, Mary Smeeth and, very importantly, Julia Swindells, with whom I wrote an early draft of the Introduction. I am also grateful to Valerie Malcolm's family for agreeing that her piece should be included here, following her death earlier this year which shocked and saddened everyone who knew her.

Grandmothers, mothers and friends of the women writing here have also put time and energy into this book, and to these women of all generations our thanks are due. What remains is for me to express quite simply my admiration for the women who have written this book, many under extremely difficult circumstances – in hospital, with small children, under pressure of other work and other deadlines – to produce what I feel is an invaluable contribution to our understanding of contemporary feminism.

Introduction

This project began with a concern to reflect on the eighties, not simply as an exercise in constructing fictions of decades – such as the 'roaring twenties' or the 'swinging sixties' – but because this period coincides with the uninterrupted reign of the Thatcher government. What has this meant for women? And for feminist politics?

There have of course been a number of events and publications which have given accounts of 'Two Decades of Feminism', and indeed much speculation about 'What is Feminism?' in the light of this history – mostly by women who have had twenty years to think about it, be part of it, and at the same time seem to stand for it. At the end of the eighties, when notions of 'women' as an unified group, of a 'common oppression', and of universal sisterhood and solidarity have so radically been called into question from within the movement by women conscious of the differences in their oppression as women – particularly Blackwomen, working-class women, lesbians, women with disabilities – we have to ask ourselves *whose* history is being represented in this way.

It is understandable that for some of those who have lived through the Britain of the sixties and seventies there is a return to that history for models of political activism. And it is no wonder that, at a superficial level, the Women's Liberation Movement of the post-'68 decade looks to those women who were involved in it as if it offered possibilities for dramatic and rapid change which no longer seem available. Much of the nostalgia, however, is for a fiction which misrepresents the historical and international complexity of that movement as much as it denies possibilities for political activism in the present. One of the more damaging consequences of this impulse towards nostalgia is the exclusion of younger women's experience in the name of a model which has had its day and cannot be repeated. Mary Smeeth writes here of the unmitigated gloom with which her 'reckless enthusiasm' for feminism was greeted in the eighties:

Wide-eyed in my brave new world, I was impatient to learn. But as I began to look around, I was at first disconcerted and then dismayed by what I found. Having set off for a party, I seemed to have arrived at a funeral. My cheerfulness was out of place – *I* was out of place.

This kind of inexorable fatalism denies the continuity of women's struggle and refuses to those who have not lived through the seventies the right to determine their own relation to the Women's Liberation Movement and its recent history.

The particular set of problems, then, that have come to light at this time are those of a feminist 'generation gap', not only that between older and younger, but between those 'first generation' feminists and those who, whatever their age, have come to feminism more recently. Norah Al-Ani's first encounter with feminism shows how absolutely essential it is for women theorising feminism, and women involved in established feminist organisations, to recognise and respond to the perspectives of other and younger women. Her first piece in this book is written from a position of total exclusion, invisibility and marginalisation, in her role as cleaner at a Women's Centre. With all their theories of inclusiveness and non-hierarchical working, the feminists running the Centre cannot 'see' Norah and the problem of their relation to her. She has to take the initiative, insisting that women on the collective take on board what she has to say. Only after this is she able to see herself as a full member of the Centre, active in it, responsible for it, identifying with it. This is symptomatic of the way in which many groups of women feel unable to identify themselves as 'feminists', where feminism means impeccable things on paper but in practice excludes Black women, working-class women, disabled women and now a younger generation of women without an audible voice.

It is not simply a question of 'including' younger and different women's perspectives in the prevailing discourse of the publishing generation of feminists, but of actively making room for them to be part of formulating feminist theory and shaping a feminist politics for the nineties. Many of the women writing here see older feminists as naive (or wilful) in their failure to make the connection between theory and practice, and here again Norah voices, from within the Women's Centre, the often exasperated engagement with much feminist work by diverse groups of women who have gone on challenging its exclusions and assumptions, sustained by a belief in what a feminist politics could be:

Dare I say it, but wouldn't it be easier working somewhere that blatantly admits it's a bastard of a system, at least you'd feel justified to just spit in its face, but working somewhere that wants to be fair and caring but finds it hard to do so . . . it's like potty-training a child, you know you hate them shitting on the Persian rug, but you know they're trying and that they might make it to the potty in time next time!

Not only have the women writing in this book grown up in the eighties; feminism has grown up in this period too.

4 SURVIVING THE BLUES

Younger women come to feminism with a particular commitment to change, one unclouded by false hopefulness and unrealistic expectations. They look at the history of the WLM in terms of the present reality of Thatcher's Britain, which pours contempt on women, erodes women's rights, and has cajoled, coaxed and ultimately pushed women back into low-paid work and onerous family responsibilities without state support. And this is their distinctive view, from the present to the future.

The women writing here do not falsely presume that their personal histories might be representative of 'young women's experience today', but show instead an acute awareness of both what is specific to their individual circumstances and what is specific to them as members of a larger group, including their gender group – women. They operate within, and have been part of creating, the more complex feminist understanding of the eighties: one which recognises and respects diverse and compounded forms of oppression; one which calls for a politics of self-determination and coalition, moving away from the impasse to which identity politics has led us. This signifies a shift in the direction which June Jordan has described as away from 'modes of being' towards 'modes of doing' – away from hierarchies of oppression. It also represents a shift away from the desire for a definitive theoretical viewpoint towards an emphasis on process, a concern with 'issues and methods' which the Spare Rib Collective sees as central to the development of a new political vision:

Issues and methods – as defined by different groups of women for themselves – are for us an integral part of a global political movement, especially at this time in history. It is about the politics of self-determination. Self-definition and self-determination are about women speaking for themselves, defining our own oppression, and setting the agenda for our liberation struggle. It entails respect for difference and the will actively to reject and break down the inevitable hierarchy and power structure which develops when one group of women speaks for another.

An emphasis on activism rather than theory is central to many of the pieces here. For Emma Wallis, Jayne Kelly and Clare Ramsaran, these tough political campaigns – Women Against Pit Closures, Stop the Clause, Greenham – can be celebrated in terms of the number of people they mobilised, and in the very act of resistance itself as a collective political protest in the face of an ideology of competitive individualism. The miners' strike was defeated and Stop the Clause did not prevent Section 28 from becoming law; yet in spite of anger and disappointment at these injustices, there is no apparent cynicism here in the face of Tory triumphalism. Winning and losing, success and failure, are not measured by these women in terms of the dominant political discourse of Thatcherism, but as a lived experience of solidarity, void of romanticism, in the context of political struggle.

One of the most striking things about many of the pieces here is that they come out of an individual experience which carries the force of a collective one. They come out of that radical activity which is often difficult and lonely, and has been particularly so in the eighties. They come out of radical lives.

Amongst the many illusions marketed by Thatcherism is that it creates space for 'the individual', regardless of gender, and supports 'the family'. The illusion of support is sustained entirely at the level of ideology; in reality, as Agnes Quashie points out, institutionalised racism, including immigration laws, operates against many families; in reality *women* support individuals (i.e. men) and in turn receive virtually no state support for their families, no encouragement to function as individuals in their own right outside the home.

The eighties promised what they could not deliver – rewards for all who went along with the 'enterprising' spirit of the times. For Mandy, having arrived at the Thatcherite goal of 'normality' – motherhood, a mortgage and a marriage whose 'success' rose and fell with the interest rates – the whole edifice of materialistic values on which this 'ideal' rests begins to fall apart:

I started an Open University course in, of all things, Women's Studies – it was the fatal blow; it only confirmed the feminist views that I had gradually begun to feel comfortable with . . . Of course money was important, but I no longer felt happy about selling my soul for it; I was starting to feel some sort of self-worth.

For Valerie Malcolm, the tangible effects of Thatcherism, the devastating changes wrought by privatisation, are brought home by a latter day visit to hospital. This time, unlike earlier visits, not only are the wards short-staffed, but the cleaning and catering have been contracted out, rendering effective health care almost impossible under these circumstances. Her experience shows that some things can never be 'profitable', can instead only be degraded by cost-cutting to serve the tyranny of the market.

Profitability is the keynote of Thatcher's Britain, and in Mary Smeeth's account, 'the '80s sold what they had while they could'. The irony is of course that most women don't have anything to sell (apart from their bodies and 'souls'), and in the labour market they still have no choice but to take low-paid jobs in intolerable conditions, like those in the wire factory where Emma Wallis worked as a welder. Unemployment is a stark reality for most of these women in their adolescence. Ruth McManus, growing up in Dumbarton, recognises early on that: 'Many mature men would never get a job again, many women would take up gruelling employment in the local distillery. But us lot, the young teenagers, had to deal with the prospect of *never* getting a job. (I still haven't got one ten years on.)' Moreover, unemployment for women is seen – by the mainstream media, the government, and popular prejudice – as infinitely less significant than for men, and fundamental gender attitudes and practices concerning work seem scarcely to have changed this century, let alone during the past decade. Norah and Louise, whose employers are worlds apart, nevertheless find themselves up against the same old stereotypes of women who do other people's shit-work. Emma finds that no matter how physically arduous her work, she is still not seen as a *real* welder, and she still can't match up to the immutable image of the miner as archetypal working-class hero.

For Emma there was an overriding sense, in the face of pit closures in South Yorkshire, of the need, as a community with high unemployment, 'to fight together to prevent the situation getting any worse'; yet she is vividly conscious of the particular oppression of women within that community. In the same way, where Ruth McManus and Louise Donald point up the oppression of the Scots by the English, they are still, as women, battling with the particular machismo of their own culture. For Louise, the sexual categories and restrictions imposed on women in Wishaw, a small town in Scotland, are simply replaced – or rather, compounded – by the scarcely subtler racism and bigotry of aspiring literati at university in England:

Wishaw had led me to believe that my sights, as befitting a woman, should remain at some ill-defined but lowly level. I imagined that university would liberate me. I was nervous, but confident. I was greeted with a different sort of diminishment, and my sense of self seriously faltered.

The question of whether education can offer routes out of oppression recurs throughout this book. The British education system is an institution which all the women here have encountered in one form or another as a privilege, as a problem, or as offering the possibility of something better. Its meaning, and its uses for them, seem to depend largely on their route into it (or out of it). For Norah, weighing the cost, it can only be something to escape from; for Ruth McManus, coming from Dumbarton via Glasgow, there is the double challenge of making sense of academic feminism and life in the South of England; for Sharmila Mukerji, higher education is simply an assumed progression from school; whereas for Chris Pegg and Emma Wallis it is something to return to and to fight for against massive odds – something which stands as an ambition to be realised.

Sharmila is not only acutely aware of her own educational privilege, a privilege which has 'shielded' her from racism; she is also clear about the limitations of higher education as a solution in itself to the problems of social isolation and the consequences for women of Thatcher's policies in the areas of employment, housing, state benefits, and civil rights in general. She reminds us that going into the academy can frequently be part of an opportunistic career route:

The policies of the Thatcher government do not encourage education for its own sake, as an education for life; rather they are concerned with the profitability of the educated people: how they can contribute towards building up the wealth and efficiency of our country, which will then be concentrated in the hands of the few who have helped to achieve this.

In one sense Sharmila has the luxury of choice, in being equally well qualified for medicine as for dance; she opts for dance in the full knowledge that in Thatcher's terms this is foolishness, because of the unprofitability of the activity. She also has no illusions about training as a contemporary dancer in a culture which is not only saturated in degrading images of women's bodies, but has censored or marginalised any medium which attempts to say anything interesting about the contemporary world.

Other women writing here do not see their experience of

education as determined in any way directly by the policies of the Thatcher government. Alison Bark makes it clear in her piece that 'fashionable ideas' about integrating pupils with disabilities in so-called 'normal' schools, theoretical ideas which cut across party politics, do not necessarily serve the best interests of these children. Schools catering for special needs, whilst academically less challenging, can provide far greater opportunities for students to participate in sport and drama, and to develop their own skills and interests. For Alison, a feminist perspective is the logical outcome of a recognition of the absurdity of prejudices against people because of the bodies they inhabit.

All the women writing here have a particular consciousness of the difference in their experience as women, over and beyond their particular circumstances and their sense of the effects of Thatcherism in general. Thatcherism is only one aspect of their growing up, and one which clearly has a different significance depending on where they are placed, geographically and economically. Jacqueline McCafferty places this decade very firmly in a larger time-scale, setting Thatcher's policies with regard to Northern Ireland in a continuum of British atrocities towards the Irish over 800 years. The Spare Rib Collective insist on placing women's struggle for liberation in a history which refuses the simple juxtaposition of '70s and '80s feminism in Britain.

This book will be an inspiration to many women, but the particular challenge – or encouragement – this book offers to feminists of an older generation is not just in terms of the powerful evidence it provides of the fact that feminism is alive and well, but a reminder that younger women are the future of the movement. Sharmila states this quite directly when she says: 'It is us who will carry forward or initiate the ideology of the future'. Just as Elizabeth Robins thought about those younger women who, in 1924, recognised the dangers of 'post-suffragism' and continued the struggle against limitations manufactured to perpetuate inequality and injustice, so should we think about women who have come to feminism in the '80s:

These girls and women, like those that came before, are being moulded by limitation on every side . . . There is a section of the new generation which, as has been noted, *does* recognise the limitation as artificially maintained. This is the section that will make history.

The very different pieces in this collection have this in common: they show the survival of feminist consciousness against the odds. I believe this to be an inspiringly strong testimony both to the individual women concerned and to feminist politics themselves for their ability to survive the most reactionary of governments, the most systematically installed of prejudices. The women writing here were no more than eighteen years old – and some as young as eight – when Thatcher came to power in 1979. For them it has hardly been a 'Golden Age', but their account of the private and public battles they have waged during this decade fuels the need, articulated quite directly by Mary Smeeth, for feminism to 'stop mourning the past, and to start listening to the future'.

Joan Scanlon, London,
February 1990

1

'Don't Ask Her, She's Just the Cleaner'*

Written and lived through by

Norah Al-Ani

When I first started working at the Centre I was fourteen. My aunt asked me one day if I'd like to earn a little pocket money doing some cleaning at her workplace.

I knew nothing about the Centre; I'd never even heard of it before. I started work assuming that my aunt had employed me and that she was my boss, but as time went on – approximately six months – I discovered quite accidentally that the Centre was non-hierarchical and a co-operative.

With this new-found information I was thrown into confusion: (1) Who was I answerable to? (2) Who paid my wages? (3) Who do I complain to? As time went by the more frustrating the job became. Although I was only there for an hour a day, that was sufficient time to realise that I was a very insignificant member of the Centre. I was never told anything. I'd always be the last one to know when the Centre was shut, when people borrowed the cleaning equipment, etc. It wasn't

* This was written in 1987 and addressed to the collective of the Women's Resources Centre where I still work. Some things have changed since then, and the piece which follows deals with a longer period of my life up to the present.

until I'd been there a year that, again by mere accident, I found out that men were not permitted to enter the building.

It became quite an adventure finding things out in this way.

Cleaning is one of the world's most hideous jobs – I HATE IT. If it weren't for the money I'd have left exactly one day after I'd started! When you do it nobody notices, but when you don't everybody does. It's positively degrading picking up other people's sanitary towels from the floor and scraping out the bottom of a dustbin after someone has thrown up in it.

I found myself apologising for being in a room, for using the hoover. I constantly felt in everyone's way. I felt too inadequate ever to join in a conversation concerning the Centre. There were also physical difficulties with the job. I would sometimes miss my last bus home simply because I was too afraid to ask people to leave a room because I wanted to clean it. As the Centre is an informal place people would come in late, in distress or just for a chat, and there followed the birth of the art of cleaning around people – one of the world's most frustrating things ever to exist.

There came a point, approximately one year later, when I began to feel unneeded. I was convinced that someone, somewhere, felt that my job was a waste of time and money.

There followed the skiving stage. A period of time in which I couldn't, or maybe wouldn't, bring myself to go within a mile of the Centre. What with thinking no one appreciated my work and worrying that I was to be got rid of.

I was bitterly ashamed of my job and the Centre for a long time. When people asked me what I did, I'd say 'a bit of this and a bit of that'. When the question arose as to where I did it, the reply would be 'in an office'. I didn't know what went on in the Centre and so felt stupid if asked questions about it.

I had always considered my job as the lowest of the low, and knew that's how the world viewed it. All the old stereotypes come to mind: Mrs Mop, no brains required for the job, only thick people cleaned up other people's shit for money. Miserable middle-aged women unfit for anything else.

At first I went into the job knowing and accepting these views, but in no time at all I'd burn up inside when women looked at me in the same way they'd look at the contents of the toilet I was cleaning.

The thing I hated most – and still do – is not feeling a part of anything, not knowing who the people were that I cleaned up after, and most of all feeling guilty about asking for my wages. But above all I hated not knowing who to turn to when someone or something upset me, and so my dearest and most loyal friend, who stuck by me through all my ordeals, the hoover, suffered badly! I have lost count of how many times I damaged the hoover out of frustration. It wasn't much of a listener.

One such incident stands out in my memory. I was hoovering the big room upstairs and feeling very sorry for myself about not being able to do anything better than clean. The more I hoovered, the more angry I got about everything. I stubbed my toe on a chair and before I could think I'd picked up the hoover and was just about to throw it through the window. It was held above my head ready for off when I remembered it cost £11 to replace a windowpane and I earned only £10.

I never really truly considered myself as a worker. I can never see myself up there with the teachers, co-ordinator this and co-ordinator that, and I say 'up there' because that's what it looks like from where I'm standing. After all, I am only there for an hour a day. My JOB is important but me, Norah, I am replaceable in a flash. My job may be as important as teaching, but the teacher is more important than me.

Some of these thoughts are stated in the past tense, but many – maybe too many – are stated in the present tense.

Meanwhile time passes, approximately three years, and one fine day my little world of cleaning is turned on its head. What's this I hear, people actually taking the time and trouble to explain things to me, all those unanswered questions of many moons ago! With amazement I hear people speak in my defence. Is that the sound of concern I hear in the distance? For the first time the centre spotlight was on *me*!

Everybody 'understands'. They have done all along, but just forgot to let me know. I am asked my opinion on things, which I forgot I had. Compliments come my way: 'Why, this is not just a job, it's an art form in disguise!' Is that a thank you I hear struggling to make itself heard over the hoovering? And to put the cherry on the top of the cake ... A PAID HOLIDAY!

With all my new-found fame and fortune came knowledge! Oh that wonderful milk of life I'd been waiting for from my first day! Knowledge handed to me on a silver plate. What more could I want? ... TO HAND IT ALL RIGHT BACK!

Oh yes, I got what I'd been screaming for: 'All you ever wanted to know about the Centre but were afraid to ask'. And how wonderful it all looked on paper and how magical it all sounded. The ideals, the aims, the very roots of the place I'd been working in for so long. Oh yes, it was all so enlightening, I would almost go as far as to say it was a spiritual experience, but I won't!

Equality for all women amongst women. The chance to relax and be yourself, express yourself with no fear of ridicule. Non-hierarchical, 'everybody is as significant and important as the next woman'. It's all very lovely on paper if you don't look too closely.

But one question remains: if all these policies and ideals founded the Centre and nurtured it, then why oh why have I just written the last three pages? Surely I couldn't have imagined it all, could I?! It's harder now than ever it was, simply because of having the knowledge that the Centre states that it intends to do one thing and yet never quite seems to follow it through.

Dare I say it, but wouldn't it be easier working somewhere that blatantly admits it's a bastard of a system, at least you'd feel justified to just spit in its face, but working somewhere that wants to be fair and caring but finds it hard to do so ...

it's like potty-training a child, you know you hate them shitting on the Persian rug, but you know they're trying and that they might make it to the potty in time next time!

I might just say that despite everything I've said, I think I can find a place in my heart for the old place, and I know I've been treated fairly well and am grateful for the wage I got from it. Maybe I could write another essay one day about all the good times I've had. But it's so hard to see things – anything – nicely when you're standing knee-deep in other people's crap.

But with my hand on my heart I can say that one of the nicest things ever to come out of the Centre are some of the people; to hear them thank me and be comforting means more to me than my hoover, and that's really saying something. But the one thing I've come to realise more and more over the years is that cleaning is important – it's a bastard, but it's as important as almost anything – but the people who do it aren't.

So there you have it: what happened, what didn't happen, what I got, but most of all what I want – forgot to mention it earlier: to work on reception . . .

2

No Going Back

Norah Al-Ani

I was born and lived for the first ten years of my life in Kirkuk, a town in the north of Iraq. I was born to an Irish mother and an Iraqi father. In 1979, the year before we came to England, I was totally oblivious of the changes that were taking place in my life. As a nine-year-old child whose biggest worry in life was whether I could stay the night at my friend's house again, I was happily going along unaware of my mother's turmoil and plans of getting herself and her daughters out of a country whose culture was too powerful for her to take on alone. At this time my sisters were also becoming increasingly aware of the changes expected from them as they embarked on puberty, in a society where puberty was a taboo subject.

We had a holiday planned that summer; my mother, sisters and I were going to England for a break, only this really was to be the 'holiday of a lifetime' – for we were never to return to Iraq. When we arrived in England, my mother calmly broke the news to us: 'We're not going back'. I thought my life had ended.

Never to return to the country I was born in, where my father, family and friends were; the place I lived, went to school, was brought up in; never to return to the only home I knew. That's what it meant to me then. For I had not yet turned the inevitable corner that my sisters had, only to find that the country we called home was to end our 'lives' the minute we were born because we were female, to find the culture we were brought up in rated women as fourth-class citizens, after men, children and animals.

So here we were, in England, with nothing more than the clothes we stood in and the few we had brought with us. I had heard adults in Iraq speak of England with great excitement: England, London, the land of prosperity, modern lifestyles, a free society, a culture that did not restrict any man, woman or child from doing as they pleased. It was spoken of as a country where people came to be educated. England, the place to be.

So I tried to comfort myself by thinking that at least we were in 'Wonderland', where everything was bigger and better. It gave me something to hold on to. But in the next year all my illusions about England were to be shattered.

We all lived with my aunt for a while in her overcrowded house. Then my mother, one sister and I left my two eldest sisters at my aunt's and moved into a small flat, but when what little money we had ran out the three of us moved in with my cousin, her husband and their new baby. Finally, after months of fighting, the council moved us into a small house with no bathroom and only a toilet in the garden.

Through the eyes of a ten-year-old my mother had brought us to a country that had nothing to offer except hardship and poverty. She had taken us from our home and brought us to . . . what? To live in a house I had naively thought was a thing of decades ago, to be read about in history books, not lived in in 1981. I could not understand my eldest sister's relief at being in England; to me the whole move had been a devastating mistake. I was determined to go back 'home' – there was nothing for us here, nothing made sense to me. It wasn't until a few years later that I was to understand why my mother had done it, and then I was able to thank her for it, but at the time there seemed no reasonable explanation.

By now we were 'settled'. It was time for us all to be put into school. I had always hated school; it wasn't a rare occurrence for me to be dragged to school screaming.

I was put in a small primary school near our house. The shock of a different schooling system set me back instantly. My problems with the language were enormous, as I had spent all my school days studying in Arabic. There was no extra help given to me, so that eventually I just slipped further and further back. I was expected to fit in and get on with it. Most of the other children's perception of my background was what they had seen in 'Carry On' films and Turkish Delight adverts.

It was at this school that I had my first taste of racism; I was horrified and shattered by it. My biggest upset was that I felt that I had to let everyone at school in Iraq know that the British didn't like them, as everyone at that school adored the English. I was very upset that the same fond feelings were not forthcoming from my new class 'mates'.

I never talked about Iraq at school and never made any reference to my past. I dedicated my time to learning as much as I could about what other class members talked and laughed about. I denied my identity by day and planned ways to get back to Iraq by night.

By now I was more convinced than ever that my mother had made a big mistake. If I hadn't held on to the hope that some day we'd be able to go back, I'd never have been able to struggle through everyday life. By this time my academic skills were rapidly deteriorating. The more red pen that was scribbled over my work, the more I withdrew. I was expected to come up to the standards of children who had spent all their school days in the British education system.

My days at school were now spent avoiding humiliating situations with teachers who still believed that 'showing children up' was the best way to get them to improve.

War had now broken out between Iraq and Iran. I had little understanding of the political situation, but its effect on me was still devastating; it meant my chances of getting back grew slimmer with every bullet that was fired. We assumed it would be over in a couple of months, but as it dragged on it was slowly destroying my hope of returning. The publicity it received left us not knowing the truth. For the British media the novelty was soon to wear off, and we would be lucky to hear anything about it from one month to the next. I couldn't even bear to think what might be happening to our family. The way the media portrayed it made it look like no one was left alive in either country after a few months of fighting.

It was now time for me to go to a secondary school and start all over again, hiding and denying my nationality for fear of persecution, and playing down my academic difficulties for fear of ridicule.

By now we had moved house again. Our new place was bigger than our last one and had an indoor toilet and a bathroom. The council had moved us into a street that did not welcome a single woman with four daughters, obviously not of British descent – but was there a street anywhere that would have welcomed a single mother with four daughters? It was at this time that I was becoming increasingly aware of the difficulties faced by women both in this country and in Iraq.

My mother's struggle to get work, to support us, drained her totally. She had no time for herself, she could never show her true feelings to us, she could never share her doubts and fears about having made this enormous move. She had to push those doubts to the back of her mind; there was no turning back now. I, on the other hand, was still convinced I could return, despite the ongoing war.

My difficulties with the work were spotted eventually by the school. I was dealt with in the way so many school-children are: I was sent to 'Remedial Class' . . . We would be called out of class and openly humiliated in front of everyone;

we were instantly labelled and any hope of improvement was knocked out of us once and for all. I was becoming increasingly aware that the British education system had no constructive way of helping children who had been in the system all their school days, let alone those from various different backgrounds with vastly different needs.

Towards the end of my first year we were asked to write an essay on our views of ourselves and our school. I freely voiced my opinion of the school, its unjust treatment of children with learning difficulties, who usually/coincidentally came from working-class families, or 'broken homes' as they were readily labelled. I also expressed my unhappiness about being in this country, not realising that I was signing away the next two years – to be spent seeing a child psychiatrist. My essay was held back and shown to a social worker, who then sent me to see a child psychologist, where I was to spend my Friday afternoons, being poked and prodded and having stereotypical diagnoses thrown at me.

Meanwhile, back at school, the more 'established' I felt, the easier things were becoming with my peers, but things got harder with the teachers. I had given up working; after all, I was stupid, backward, difficult, so I was going to live up to their expectations. I spent most of my time fighting and arguing with the staff about unjust rules and regulations.

As time went by I was painfully waking up to the truth about Iraq: I could never go back, there was nothing there for me any more, the grass was no greener there than it was here. That was a very hard thing to come to terms with. I had to let go of the one thing that had kept me going all this time; I now had to open my eyes and not look at things from the point of view of a ten-year-old girl but as a young woman whose prospects might be dim in this country but would be non-existent in Iraq. Now that I had let go, I was left with the inevitable realisation that 'this was it'. I was going to have to make the best of what I had; there was nowhere to run to now. I now had to start going through what my mother must have gone through when we first arrived.

The war was still going strong, although it had stopped being reported on the news, as it was no longer 'New News'. By now I was finding that the only way I could cope with the realisation that I would never return to Iraq was by not thinking about it, trying to make my childhood there as alien to me as England had been when we first arrived. I had to put it behind me and not look back.

I found that my years of denying my identity were very damaging and left me not knowing who or what I really was. I was so busy hiding it and lying about it that I'd forgotten what I was or even what I wanted to be. I seemed to have spent my years in Iraq convincing myself and others that I was a true Arab through and through, and for the years I was here I spent all my time undoing that work and replacing it with an attempt to be as British as possible. And it's only recently that I've decided that it really doesn't matter any more. I don't have to be either, because I am both.

My school days were drawing to a close and the feeling of apathy amongst so many of us was strong. Unemployment figures were high and teachers' strikes were a common occurrence. When we all realised that we'd be thrown out into the 'big bad world' and expected to survive it, only then did we suddenly realise that if you didn't get your results and go off to college – you were finished! There was barely enough employment for the 'educated' population, let alone thousands of young school leavers with barely a CSE to their name. Yet again the more divisions were made between us, the more we realised that's what it had all been about; those of us who didn't make it were not given a second thought. The school merely needed their yearly statistics of passes and didn't pay any attention to those of us who were left to slip to the back of the class.

I was devastated when I left school. I had spent eleven years of my life there and hated every minute of it, but I had completely missed the whole point. I attempted to go to a Further Education College but very quickly realised that I could not bear to spend any more of my life in an education system that only valued certificates as a sign of intelligence and gave no value to individual quality. So I left, making one of the biggest decisions of my life so far. I now had to live with the consequences, knowing that I'd have to prove myself twice as hard as someone who had stuck it out, and having to live with the fact that other people's estimation of me would be very low when they realised my lack of recognised qualifications.

I had by this time been working as a cleaner in a Women's Centre, where I was also doing English classes which helped me build up what had been knocked out of me at school – confidence and the belief that I *was* capable of achieving something. As much as the Centre 'gave to me' it ironically 'took from me' by my doing the cleaning there. At first it meant little to me, the fact that I was doing the cleaning. It was just a job, but as time went by I realised that I was doing all that was to be expected of me, again. I was simply doing menial work that involved no brainpower. As my personal beliefs developed, as far as working in a feminist organisation goes, I could no longer see it as just a job but as a political issue.

I have since started working in a different capacity at the Centre and we no longer employ cleaners; all women who use the Centre are responsible for the cleaning of it.

The Centre has helped to change my life: it has given me a place of work without having to produce reams of qualifications; I am taken as I am for the work I do. And for me to see many young women coming into the Centre in the position I found myself in a few years ago only makes me wish I'd 'found' it when we first arrived in this country.

There is no looking back now; I no longer deny myself or my past; and although I left school without the standard

recognised qualifications, I left with much, much more ...
the will to fight and continue. And my working at the
Women's Centre has given me back my sight to see my own
self-worth – as an Irish Arab and as a woman.

3
Can You Hear Me at the Front?

Mary Smeeth

Commodity Politics

Will 'the '80s' be a sellable product soon? What would be the souvenirs? A GLC pencil case, perhaps, a '10 More Years' Tory poster, a Falklands War medal? Is anyone interested, does anyone care? It is my belief that the '80s sold what they had while they could. I think this will be the most disowned decade of the twentieth century. It seems that everyone has either sold up or sold out. The 'yuppies' are heading straight for the door or the Shetland Islands, and those who remain are little more than a tired and rather pathetic joke. Even Mrs Thatcher is looking shaky.

In a recent article in *The Mail on Sunday*, Julie Burchill bemoaned the approach of the 'nice '90s'. Designer families and green consumerism are on the way in; narcissistic individuals and 'spend, spend, spend' are long gone. Should we be pleased – should we, like the East Berliners, be dancing in the street? Is this revolution? Of course not.

The culture we live in is dominated by fashion, and there is nothing more unfashionable than being 'into' the old designer trends. So hide your Filofax and whip out your recycled notepad instead. Wear your Greenpeace badge with pride, but don't go to Greenham Common – it's a mad, bad, sad place and there isn't a wine bar for miles. Oh yes, you can still go to wine bars, but drink only Perrier Water (*not* tap water) and don't smoke anything unless it's your free-range herring.

Everyone except the Labour Party seems to have cottoned on to the fact that the only good thing about the '80s is that they are over. Ironically, Labour might win the next election by virtue of being out of office for the entire 'yuppie' period. (I said *might*.) Spurious attempts to impose an 'authorised version' of events are made by the media every year-end. The end of *ten* years must seem irresistible. Photomontage-type coverage necessarily proliferated in media text and image, relentlessly pursuing us through Christmas and into 1990. The Falklands War veteran without a face pasted over Charles's and Di's wedding pics; shots of 'the riots' next to Edwina Currie and some eggs; a miners' picket line blending into a city whizzkid stepping out of a Porsche. What a mess. The public face of a decade under a government that set no limits on how far it would go or how low it would sink. And yet, inevitably, for most of us who lived through the '80s, it 'wasn't like that'. We may have been caught up in one particular public event, but for the rest, the terrible truth is that they registered as little more than a backdrop to our daily lives.

The Great Escape

The most positive experience I had in the '80s was discovering feminism. It, as they say in all the worst commercials, 'changed my life'. When I arrived at university – midterm for Thatcher, first term for me – I was twenty-three. With two Lloyd Cole tapes and a selection of baggy black jumpers I thought I was dead sophisticated. This illusion lasted right up to the first seminar. Everyone seemed to either be, or be intimately connected to, someone 'incredibly famous'. And of course everyone had been to public school. Talk about gob-smacked! I nearly left that day. I didn't, though. I got drunk instead. Just me and Lloyd Cole and a bottle of vodka. I cried a bit and walked up and down my room – which took about two seconds (the first time I saw it, I thought it must be a walk-in closet [sic]). Feeling so different from everyone else, so apart, led me to picture myself wandering around campus alone: a melancholy, almost tragic figure. I was deeply moved. I felt better almost immediately. Little did I suspect that all around me, in hundreds of little cells like mine, other 'freshers' were enacting initiation ceremonies almost identical to my own. So much for the poetic imagination.

To cut a long and boring story short, I sought solace from the spectre of academic and social failure in what I loosely termed relationships. The AIDS-conscious era had yet to arrive, and although I thought I was getting to be more selective, I still seemed to be waking up to quite a few men who could have landed immediate walk-on parts in *Planet of the Apes*. I didn't mind the sex so much – although the average stud's idea of foreplay was taking his trousers off – it was the conversation that really got me down. Honestly, I've had more intellectual stimulation from reading the back of a cornflakes packet.

I warily considered joining the Women's Group, but I didn't fancy it somehow. It was a group I regarded half with contempt and half with awe. It seemed like such a closed society. What did those 'wimmin'' do, I wondered. My friend said she 'knew for a fact' that they were all lesbians. (If only she'd been right!) I had some vague notion of the 'wombyn' – spelling didn't seem to be their strong point – synchronising their menstrual rhythms and making womb music. And I wondered, too, what it would be like to be born a lesbian. Pretty awful, I imagined. I had seen 'two of them' in the coffee bar and met 'one' in a class, so I knew what they were like: mental. Of course, like almost every other straight woman who thought she was a feminist/alternative person, I had my quota of gay male friends who I thought were 'sweet'. But that was different – very different from the unknowable sub-species: Lesbian.

Then, one day, the consequences of being even a titchy bit feminist were brought home to me. I found myself in the middle of a nasty row about sexism in a feminist theory seminar. Front-line stuff! In a light-hearted way I had chipped into a debate on the women's side. In response to the demand: 'When, when were we sexist?' I had done what I thought at the time to be a rather hilarious and inoffensive impression of a man talking across a hitherto silent and very nervous younger woman. To say that the response was frosty would hardly cover it. I had committed the ultimate sin: hurt a man's feelings. And not just any man – this was a *new* man. He was trying really hard and all he got was criticism. Suddenly, the women's side became the woman's – mine. I was cast as a 'strong woman' – fearless, and therefore open to any kind of offensive behaviour anyone felt like doling out. It went, it seemed, with the territory. The sisters? I couldn't see them for dust. I guess they saw me as a head on a spike and weren't too crazy about going the same way.

What's a girl to do? I tramped around a bit, feeling alternately pissed off and nervous. I took a daily three-mile detour to avoid highly populated areas of campus. I gloomily monitored the way the affair had become 'famous'. The Socialist Workers had a caucus and bonded with the new men; the new men bonded with each other and the 'old' men. It was a very bonding experience (for others). There was even a 'Masculinity Forum' set up, to provide a safe space for male bonding away, presumably, from the castrating glare of 'that cow'.

What happened next was down to damage limitation – and luck. If male approval was so conditional, it seemed unlikely that I would ever get it back. And even if I did, what sort of person would I be? I didn't have anything to lose – I became a lesbian. Of course this was a process over time – about twenty-four hours, I recall. Once I had been informed that you weren't 'born like that', you chose it, I was in. Who wouldn't be? It no longer seemed mental but, rather, super-sane. I suppose it depends where you're standing. Maybe I should credit the woman who volunteered the information about lesbianism that I needed to hear – i.e. that (a) being a lesbian isn't a medical condition, and (b) lesbians get to have much more fun. But I think, to be fair, that at least some of the credit for my quick (but long overdue) exit from heterosexuality should go to the new men. And I never looked back.

These events took place at a small campus university, where you couldn't pick your nose without it being written up in the local press. The outraged response to my 'perverted' defection was wonderful to behold, especally in the New Man camp. Theories were quickly developed, the only printable ones being that I'd always been unstable and this just proved I was mad; and that I'd just done it to win the argument and I would, wouldn't I. A less amusing outcome was that I lost all my straight friends. This didn't happen overnight – I wish it had; at least it would have been an honest separation. My friends were more subtle, and more cruel. They waited just long enough for me to be sure of them, and for them to be sure that I wasn't redeemable, that this wasn't 'just a phase' – and then they quietly slipped away. I didn't even get to star in a big parting scene – not even with my 'best friend', especially not with her. I think that was the most depressing aspect: that something so painful should also be so very banal. *Desert Hearts* it wasn't. (I guess I should be grateful for that at least.) But even in my worst moments, I couldn't seriously imagine 'going back'. I had come too far forward, and I knew that I was – that I am – one of the lucky ones.

Feminism in the '80s: A True Story

If I tumbled into lesbian feminism with a reckless enthusiasm, my more experienced sisters could hardly be accused of giving me irresponsible encouragement – or, in fact, any sort of encouragement at all (with one honourable exception). Wide-eyed in my brave new world, I was impatient to learn. But as I began to look around, I was at first disconcerted and then dismayed by what I found. Having set off for a party, I seemed to have arrived at a funeral. My cheerfulness was out of place – *I* was out of place. As well as discomfort, I felt more than a little chagrin that everyone appeared to be saying goodbye to feminism when I'd barely been introduced. The following statements are typical:

We have had nothing but criticism of the labour movement over the last six or seven years from feminists. Yet feminists do not seem to have found a way of dealing with disagreements among themselves.
(Elizabeth Wilson, 1986[1])

This article is being written at a time of depression and lack of confidence in feminist politics . . .
(Ardill and O'Sullivan, 1986[2])

There has been no national [Women's Liberation] conference since 1978. WIRES, the national newsletter, is no longer being published. Infighting is at an all-time high.
(Sigrid Nielson, 1987[3])

In an increasingly conservative, reactionary and anti-feminist climate, it is important not to blame feminism's 'failures' entirely on feminism itself.
(Franklin and Stacey, 1988[4])

1988/89 is a very depressing endpoint for a discussion of women's liberation politics [. . .] It tears at the heart to be asked to look back from here to times of such confidence and hope.
(Sophie Laws, 1989[5])

From such comments I gathered that in the '70s feminism had been a group activity – like sex in the '60s. Feminism in the

'80s is perceived as an individual's act of faith or struggle. I was struck by the uncomfortable thought that this denial of a current feminist politics, combined with nostalgia for the 1970s WLM (Women's Liberation Movement), colluded with the mainstream media's declaration that we were living in a 'post-feminist' era. In both cases the authorised version of the feminist position denied not only my own experience but that of a lot of other young women I knew who were highly politicised, highly motivated and highly committed to feminism. It seems significant that the only feminist magazine aimed at the youth market – *Shocking Pink* – is notably more cheerful and dynamic than its big sisters.

Private reading was not the only alienating experience; public events proved just as inhospitable. At the (in)famous Lesbian Summer School, for example, it was obvious that a number of participants thought us 'youngsters' should have been left in the crèche. Faced with our continued presence, it was deemed best to ignore it.

Example

I am in a room with women of all ages. A '70s Sister' (SS) is leading a workshop. Someone asks her if *Spare Rib* is a 'politically correct' read. 'Good God(ess)!' – the SS explodes, curling an eyebrow and raising a lip. 'Does ANYONE – ' she adds sarcastically ' – still read *Spare Rib*? I thought everyone gave it up in the '70s!' Well, that would have involved quite a few of us in the room making that decision aged about ten. Picture the scene: 'Look Mum, I've told you before – stop packing *Spare Rib* in my lunch box. It's embarrassingly passé – I'm in Junior School now, you know, not big infants.' I'm not ruling this out as a possible childhood experience, but I'd say it was unlikely.

Discovering feminism in 1986 rather than in 1976 or even 1966 may seem weird, but it happens, it happened. So to go on pretending that everyone involved in feminism is the same age, comes from the same background and shares the same history is not only short-sighted and stupid but destructive and insulting. What may be 'dead' for some women is just coming to life for others. But as the dirge seems unlikely to let up as we enter the '90s, it seems necessary to ask what, if anything, is lost and gone for ever.

How Was it for You?

Hardened no doubt by 'Thatcher's Britain', I have to ask: was the early WLM so fantastic? And, if it was, who was it fantastic for? I ask because we seem to have been left with a lot of shit to shovel up in the wake of second-wave feminism – a feminism based on the false premiss that differences between women were less important than what united them: men as the common enemy. What this meant in reality was that a lot of women were excluded because their oppression was being denied by women who were not oppressed in the same way. This kind of 'women's liberation movement' hardly constitutes a Golden Age of feminism. bell hooks, a Black American feminist, summed up a lot of what was wrong in her book *From Margin to Center*, published in 1984:

The idea of 'common oppression' was a corrupt platform disguising and mystifying the true nature of women's varied and complex social reality. Women are divided by sexist attitudes, racism, class privilege, and a host of other prejudices. Sustained woman bonding can occur only when these divisions are confronted and the necessary steps are taken to eliminate them. Divisions will not be eliminated by wishful thinking or romantic reverie about common oppression despite the value of highlighting experiences all women share.[6]

We hear a lot today about how differences between women – in terms of race, class, mobility and sexuality – have split the women's movement. If it could split so easily, was it worth trying to hang on to? I do not feel sorry that I missed out on that early movement, just glad that I am part of a new feminism which can learn from past mistakes. Not, I hasten to add, that I think feminism now is particularly brilliant at dealing with difference; but at least we are able to acknowledge that women can oppress each other – the problem now being a tendency to try and out-oppress each other as a way to avoid being challenged ourselves. This, I have to say, is a very tacky practice and one that I think should be banned, especially at feminist conferences. The surest way not to deal with real power imbalances is to invent pretend ones. It is my fervent hope that in the 1990s the 'ism' war will be all played out for good.

Feminism in the '80s may seem like a very messy affair compared with what it was. It is, I suppose, messy as well as being unresolved and, at times, painful. But if it is harder to find answers now, maybe it is because we are asking better questions. As for all the wailing and gnashing of teeth from certain quarters, I think it's a little premature to throw in the towel. If I am optimistic about the future, it is not out of any perverse desire to spite my elders. I find plenty to sing about in the courage and generosity of feminists like bell hooks, who are proof that getting real doesn't mean giving up:

Women do not need to eradicate difference to feel solidarity. We do not need to share common oppression to fight equally to end oppression [. . .] we can be sisters united by shared interests and beliefs, united in our struggle to end sexist oppression, united in political solidarity.[7]

I wouldn't have missed the '80s for anything because that's when I learned to look through my own eyes, and name my own reality. It is unlikely, however, that I am ever going to treasure it as a Golden Age! I just hope that I will always remember how I feel now, and that I can fend off that tired cynicism that diminishes not only the person but the politics too. It is time, I would like to suggest, to stop mourning the past, and to start listening to the future. Can you hear me at the front?

Notes

1. 'Feminism and Class Politics: A Round-Table Discussion', *Feminist Review*, no. 23, Summer 1986, p. 24.

2. 'Upsetting an Applecart: Difference, Desire and Lesbian Sadomasochism', in *Sexuality: A Reader*, London, Virago, 1987, p. 279.

3. 'The State of the Movement: "From the Faraway Nearby"', *Trouble and Strife*, no. 11, Summer 1987, p. 55.

4. 'Dyke-tactics for Difficult Times', in *Out the Other Side: Contemporary Lesbian Writing*, ed. McEwan and O'Sullivan, London, Virago, 1988, p. 228.

5. ''68, '78, '88', *Trouble and Strife*, no. 16, Summer 1989, p. 30.

6. From an edited version of Chapter 4 of *Feminist Theory: From Margin to Center* (Boston, MA, South End Press, 1984), which appeared as 'SISTERHOOD: Political Solidarity Between Women', in *Feminist Review*, no. 23, Summer 1986, p. 127.

7. ibid, p. 138.

4

I Wouldn't Have Missed It for the World

Emma Wallis

I was born in 1965 and lived until I was eighteen in a village to the east of Rotherham. Though not a mining village in the sense of having its own pit, there were five collieries within a five-mile radius, and a high proportion of men who lived in the village were employed within the coal industry.

My immediate family had no connection with the industry. My mother was a nurse and I was brought up jointly by her and my granny and grandad, both of whom were domestic servants during their working years. Although my mother was married (not to my father, though I called him Dad) I can never remember him being around for most of the time, or having a particularly great influence on me. Not that he was a bad man – far from it, he was gentle, loving and kind; but he worked very long hours in the hospital and died when I was thirteen, my mother marrying again within the year.

I attended the local comprehensive school and passed three O levels in 1982. On reflection I wish I had tried harder, because I was capable of better results, but I hated most aspects of the school system and the only way I felt I could register a protest was by opting out altogether. In more recent years, however, I developed a desire to redeem myself educationally, and to broaden my knowledge in general. With this in mind I applied for a place on the two-year residential course in Trade Union and Industrial Studies at Northern College, where I am currently a student.

For me the most important event of the 1980s was the 1984–5 miners' strike. When the strike broke I was eighteen years old and had been living in Sheffield for several months. However, I realised the impact that large-scale closures of collieries would have on South Yorkshire. Unemployment was already high in the county owing to lay-offs in the steel industry, and being unemployed myself I felt that we all had to fight together to prevent the situation getting any worse. My mother was of the same opinion, so we both went to join the Sheffield Women Against Pit Closures group. Ironically, being unemployed was a bonus at this time, as it enabled me to do far more work with WAPC than I would have been able to do had I had a job.

I had never been involved with any political organisation or pressure group before I joined WAPC and I was very impressed with the organisation, as it was highly democratic; we all joined in the decisions, and we all took part in the many and varied activities arranged to support the strike. There were women in the group from all walks of life with differing viewpoints, perspectives and experiences, and it was wonderful how we all managed to get along with only minor disagreements.

The major function of SWAPC was to fund-raise in order that we might send money to the pits we supported. We did this in many different ways: from street collections, which I didn't really enjoy – because although for the most part the people of Sheffield supported our cause, every now and again someone would come up to be deliberately rude and offensive – to appeals, letters in newspapers, stalls at shows, badge-making and T-shirt-making. Oh those T-shirts . . . We used to buy in plain T-shirts, print them on a silk-screen machine with the

WAPC logo and then sell them, the profits going to the pits. By the end of the strike I wouldn't have minded if I never saw another T-shirt as long as I lived.

SWAPC also used to go on demonstrations and arrange pickets, and it was these particular events more than anything else which happened during the strike which affected me, as they opened my eyes to many things which I didn't realise happened in this country and caused me to reconsider my point of view on many issues.

Before the strike I had always been of the opinion that we had a fair, just and neutral police force. However, as the dispute progressed and police tactics became more violent, I began to realise that this simply wasn't the case. The police were just as violent towards us as women as they were to the men, but in addition they used to treat us with a mixture of contempt and sexual intimidation. The comment was always made that no woman worked down the pit, so we shouldn't be on the picket line but at home doing the dishes, or in bed with our husbands. They were often obscene, and frequently talked to us like dirt. In the end I grew to accept this, viewing it as part of the job. I certainly didn't stop going picketing but became very good at cheeking coppers back. The only thing that really worried me when going out picketing was the thought of being arrested whilst I was having a period. I'd heard so many tales of how the police tactic with women was to arrest them and not let them go to the loo that it really intimidated me, and I felt that being degraded in that way would be more than I could take.

It was nigh-on impossible to get into Nottinghamshire; they had roadblocks on all the motorway exits and all the main roads into the county from the North, but we still kept going when the Notts WAPC requested assistance. When we were stopped we used to tell them all sorts of tales: We've been to nightclubs, darts matches, Tupperware parties, the airport, the hospital, potato picking – and all at two or three in the morning. Sometimes they believed us, sometimes they didn't; that was the way it was.

The police tactics at the big pickets, though, were really frightening. One night in particular two of us went to Treeton. There were no police when we got there and loads of pickets, but the police soon arrived in great numbers. They came in from both sides of the village so, being in effect surrounded, we fled in the only direction we couldn't see blue flashing lights. I was separated from Audrey and somehow ended up in the middle of a field, alone, not knowing where I was. Then the police searchlights began panning out from behind me and I was on the verge of panic. I saw some hedges which looked as if they surrounded allotments, so I made my way over to them and hid out of the way of the searchlights. I knew I couldn't stay there long because most of the pickets had run in the same direction as myself so I knew the police would not be far behind. Over to my left a few hundred yards away was a small ridge with a solitary silhouette standing on top of it, so I made my way to the bottom and then climbed up, hoping the person at the top was not a policeman, although I guessed that he wasn't or he wouldn't have been alone. I guessed correctly and sat down at the top of the ridge with the man, and was shortly joined by Audrey and four other NUM members. As we looked down from the ridge we saw blue flashing lights and riot shields everywhere. We were relatively safe there, but because of the searchlights we had to lie flat for the best part of three hours before we dared attempt to leave the village. We got out via railway lines, back gardens, and with a lot of dodging police cars in between.

It was an incredible night which could have come straight out of a war film, but it happened less than ten miles from the centre of Sheffield. I doubt if I would have believed it myself had I not been there.

Trying to explain what it was like to people who weren't active in the strike was very difficult because most of the time I just wasn't believed.

The TV and press were pouring out endless streams of rubbish, yet apparently they had more credibility than I did. Looking back on it now, I can't helping thinking that if I'd been a man in, say, his mid-thirties, rather than an eighteen-year-old woman, people might not have been so dismissive of my experiences. I suppose it takes something really dramatic like, say, being at Orgreave where thousands of police in full riot gear with horses, dogs and armoured vans fought with umarmed miners who were trying to picket the coke-works, before it's possible to shake off many decades of conditioning.

To begin with, after witnessing events such as Orgreave, a very one-sided battle, and the roadblocks in Nottinghamshire and policemen lying in court in order to convict men who had done literally nothing, I felt angry and confused and hated the police with great intensity, but I also began to question our society and the assertion that Britain is a free country. In SWAPC were women from Greenham Common, and women who had contacts with the Black community and with people in Northern Ireland. After I listened to the things they had to say and the experiences they related, it began to appear to me that only people who supported the status quo were free; anyone who challenged the status quo, or even questioned it, had the powers of the state brought to bear on them. This was an idea which made me feel uncomfortable, but there has not been – nor can there ever be – a return to my pre-strike viewpoint, and I know that many women who were involved in the strike share that feeling, because for most of us it was the first time we had ever challenged the state.

I think that has to be the one good thing that came out of the strike: the politicising of many thousands of people, because wherever people went after the strike they wouldn't have been able to forget what they'd seen, because it's just impossible to be rid of images such as Orgreave; it's always there at the back of your mind.

The strike ended in March 1985. I went on the march back

at Silverwood colliery, on a cold damp morning that I don't think I'll ever forget. The weekend before the march back had been eerily quiet apart from the self-congratulatory news reports which I could hardly bear to watch. My emotions had been building up so when I heard the brass band playing in the distance a lump came into my throat, but it was when the men came under the bridge shoulder to shoulder with the banner aloft that I began to cry, and I thought I would cry for the rest of my life. I was so distressed that despite giving of our best for so long we'd been defeated, and I was angry that despite the fact that our demands were not great some bastard in Whitehall would be celebrating that we'd been beaten, and I was frightened because I knew what was going to happen to my town and its people. Everyone was crying – if not openly then inside, to themselves – but our sadness turned to anger when we saw the scabs working on the pit top. In one of the buildings some of the women noticed Longden, who'd been amongst the first to go back. He'd had a policeman stationed at his house to protect him but the policeman ran off with his wife, so when we saw him we started singing: 'Where's your missis, Mr Longden?' before he disappeared from view. The men decided not to go back that day, so we made our way home numb and upset.

Despite the fact that the strike was lost, I wouldn't have missed that year for the world, and I'd do it all again tomorrow. I learned so much – about politics, about the country I thought I knew but found I had to come to terms with all over again, about people, about myself and about comradeship. During that year the women at SWAPC had been like an extended family. We'd laughed together, cried together, been tired together and in danger together. We'd all experienced so many different things it was incredible, but for me that was the spirit of the strike – comradeship. Just one little yellow sticker, that's all it took. You could see someone you'd never met before, you wouldn't know any-thing about them, but from the moment you saw the little yellow sticker you were comrades, allies, friends, and you'd help each other.

I was still unemployed at the end of the strike, but with nothing to do I gradually got quite depressed and very, very bored. The DHSS decided to send me to a rehabilitation centre – I'm not sure why, it was a job I needed, not rehabilitating, but I was offered £38 a week instead of about £24, so off I went. I could choose from various types of work, and could spend eight weeks in one section. I decided that I wanted to go in the engineering section, because I did metalwork at school and quite fancied a job in industry. Needless to say they tried to encourage me to go into the secretarial section to learn office skills, but I refused, so I ended up in the engineering section making lecterns for disabled people. I was really happy there despite being the only woman; there was a lot of banter, but it was mostly good-humoured and besides, I felt that I was doing something useful and earning my keep. I could go for a pint on a Friday night with a clear conscience. I did a bit of electric arc and gas welding, and so when my eight weeks were up I went on a part-time course in welding at the Engineering Industry Training Board. Again I was the only woman, this time with 250-odd men, but once again I really enjoyed myself. Through this I applied to the Skillcentre in Sheffield for their six-month pipe-fitting and welding course. I knew I would probably have to wait until a place was vacant, but I was really excited because I enjoyed welding. I went for the trade test and all the time the instructor was making comments to try to put me off, such as 'We've never had a woman on this course before', and 'Most of our lads are set on by the NCB; how do you fancy a job working down the pit?' I would have liked to say that if there were any pits left I would love to work there, but took my satisfaction from the expression on his silly little face when he told me that I'd passed the trade test, and would go on the waiting list for a place on the course.

I had been unemployed for about another nine months

when a place on the course came up, but within days I was also offered a place at ROMAC (Rotherham Metropolitan Age Concern), on a Community Programme scheme. As I had been applying for jobs within the engineering industry without any success whatsoever and the place at ROMAC was for twelve months at £50 per week, whereas the pipe-fitting and welding course was for only six months at £38 per week, I took the place at ROMAC, cursing under my breath.

I worked at ROMAC from August 1986 until August 1987. There were a few women there, although the workforce was dominated by men. I started work on the painting and decorating side, but after six months I was bored with this, so I asked for a transfer to the security section and spent the rest of my time there fitting security bolts, window catches and draught-proofing in the homes of elderly people.

It was while I was at ROMAC that I joined UCATT (Union of Construction, Allied Trades and Technicians). Of course I'd wanted to be a union member long before, but on the dole it was an impossibility. I decided I wanted to be a shop steward so I went to the Branch meeting in Rotherham. I felt a little intimidated really, walking into a union meeting – a roomful of men, none of whom I knew – and telling them that I wanted to be shop steward. I might as well not have bothered because although the men at ROMAC supported me in the elections, after that they largely seemed to view me as a figure of fun: 'What do women know about unions anyway?' was an oft-repeated question. To be fair, the men at the Branch weren't much better to begin with; I don't think they trusted me and they wouldn't talk to me much.

The thing that made the difference was the 1987 general election. The Branch was asked to canvass up in Dewsbury (Rotherham being a safe seat) so I volunteered to help out. We were going up to Dewsbury a couple of times a week, and I think by the end of the campaign the men felt that I'd somehow proved myself and I became an accepted member of the Branch. In any case, Dewsbury returned a Labour MP.

I was back on the dole again in August 1987 and once again I felt bored and frustrated. I felt isolated and stigmatised and missed the collective identity of being part of a workforce. I found it very difficult to explain my feelings to other people because by this time I was living with a man I met during the strike and when I mentioned that I was unemployed people responded with 'Well, Billy's working, isn't he?' I realised that my position was not as bad as that of families with no wage-earner at all, but that really wasn't the point. People, family especially, seemed to think that unemployment wasn't as bad for women as it was for men, and couldn't seem to grasp at all the fact that I wanted to be my own independent person with my own identity rather than be someone's appendage.

Then, when I was twenty-two years old, a miracle happened. I got a job, a proper job, not a government scheme but a real job in a wire factory.

The majority of the workforce at the factory were women. Most of them were full-timers; however, I was employed as a 'temp' to work over the busy period and then be laid off again as soon as work slackened. I was, for most of the time, employed as a spot-welder, which was very hard, boring and repetitive. The electrodes were operated by a foot pedal, which was kicked down once for each weld. Each particular job had its own 'number' which meant we had to produce that amount, each hour, for eight hours, every single day. There was no bonus if you made more than was necessary, just the sack if you weren't up to scratch. This repetitive knee movement caused a lot of pain; sometimes I would cry at night because I couldn't sleep for the pain in my knee. On component 1073, for example, the number was 143 for the hour; each component had six welds, so we had to kick the pedal down 858 times an hour (6864 times a day) on that particular job, in addition to stacking the finished work in a skip and bringing mesh and wire to the table.

I often didn't know what I was making, and once told I was

frequently none the wiser, as most of the products were so nondescript it was hard to envisage them having any practical purpose whatsoever, but I was taking home nearly £70 per week, which was the most I'd ever earned, so I didn't really care. In any event the work was so monotonous that I spent most of the day with my own private thoughts. It wasn't necessary to think about the work; that just sort of happened automatically, as if we were remote-controlled.

If work slackened on our floor we were sent to either the other production floors or packing. Packing was mind-numbingly futile: just putting things in boxes all day, or in polythene bags – at least on the production floors there was an end result, something to look at at the end of the day and say 'I've made that', even if you didn't know what it was. But putting unidentifiable objects in plastic bags all day seemed a totally pointless exercise to me.

One of the other production floors was only about 30 feet wide and 100 feet long and crammed full of machinery with a small gangway just wide enough to get a skip through. It was also underground with no natural light, and incredibly noisy. I spent three horrendous weeks down there 'catching' on the guillotine. This entailed sitting on a small metal stool about six inches high so that I could catch the mesh as it came out at the back of the guillotine, and stack it in a skip. No one told me the right way to go about this, so when the first mesh came through the sharp points gashed my arms. I was continually being cut on that job because the mesh came through at such speed and because no protective clothing was made available.

The women didn't dare complain about the conditions because they would have been sacked. The management didn't recognise the union, and in an area hit by mass unemployment I think people felt they were lucky to have a job at all. The only thing that made the job bearable was the camaraderie of the women, most of whom lived within three miles of the factory. They were really friendly and everyone knew everyone else, and their business, or if they didn't they made sure they found out.

Whilst I was at the firm I made a point of staying in UCATT, although it was difficult to get over to the men how hard the work was. I think they were still of the opinion that only men work hard. My mother used to infuriate me because whenever I used to have a little grumble she used to say, 'Oh, but what about poor Billy having to spend his day down the pit.' Billy himself admitted that on balance my job was probably harder in the physical sense than his, but I still found it hard to live up to the reputation of a miner. I also found it incredibly annoying, when describing my job to one of the men I had met in the strike, to be dismissed because spot-welding wasn't 'proper welding'. I could have screamed.

UCATT enabled me to go on educational weekend schools, and these, combined with TUC courses taken whilst I was at ROMAC, made me want to further my education. When I was offered a place at Northern College I had no hesitation in giving up my job in the wire factory, and I am currently in the second year of a two-year course in Trade Union and Industrial Studies. I have enjoyed the course immensely and gained a lot of satisfaction from dealing with new ideas and concepts, and have appreciated being treated for once like a human being with my own thoughts and opinions, instead of as part of the machinery – or a government statistic.

5

Shades of Blue

Mandy Nichol

I can now look back from where I've run to and see how all that surrounded me moulded me into the person I am: the people, the place, family and friends, both in my personal life and politically. I behaved in the expected ways – maybe not successfully, but I did try. I had thought that their way was the right way for me; I now know I was wrong. Failure was to be what I feared most, in a town where failure is not conforming to the 'norm'.

I have left a prison of my own making – and that of the beautiful Galloway Hills, which overlook every move you make. The town lies in a valley of forests and lochs, a place which outsiders envy. Little do they know that to live there is like a time warp, a world of small minds and gossips.

Maybe I was a coward to leave, but I knew if I was to start any kind of new life, I had to escape. To find the thing I've been searching for, the thing I've been unable to put a name to. I do know that to have stayed would have meant suffocation, to carry on breathing but not living. I haven't liked myself very much during the past years, the years I have spent trying to do all that I thought was right. The things I had once held dear to me – my opinions, my politics – had become hidden from view to satisfy the need for security and a future for my son and me. I hadn't changed them, only shaded them for a few years. Only now I know they are more important to me than I could ever have imagined. It feels as if I had lost an old friend who has returned to me closer and stronger.

I have lived my teenage years and my married life in a climate where you think of yourself and your bank balance first and care about others second, a time when the only government I've ever experienced has been a blue one. It influenced me in my don't-give-a-damn attitude at school; there were no jobs anyway, so why spend time getting qualifications for jobs that weren't there to begin with? I thought it was smart to walk out of my exams after a few minutes. Nobody else cared, so why should I?

I thought it would be a bit of fun to go on the dole for a while; I was going to spend my days sleeping and my nights and weekends having fun. I never thought the lack of money was going to affect me in any way or form. My mum had brought my two sisters and me up by herself, a life of social security and no man to tell us what to do. She had said we had to learn from our own mistakes, so she let me get on with doing as I pleased. It was a year of no money, lazy wasted days and punk rock. But this was Thatcher's Britain. I knew I wasn't one of the go-getters so I would be one of the couldn't-care-less; after all, I had no prospects. I think eventually my mum despaired of me. She always seemed to be moaning at me. But looking back, I can see why.

After this year of wasting my time I decided to get myself a job, any kind of job, anything to give me a purpose for getting up in the morning. It was the start of the government's YTS scheme – I think we were its first guinea pigs. It was something to put all the strays into, a hole, a hole in which to hide us all and forget us. I thought anything was better than nothing, so I tried it.

The hospital I got a place in was a new world for me, £20 a

week and women, a place where words and gossip could make you or break you. I loved it; the work didn't stretch my mind but it gave me a purpose. I was eventually asked if I would like a full-time job. I owed the YTS nothing, I got that job through hard work and on my own merit. I earned good money and felt a new independence. It felt wonderful. Then the feeling of looking for something else started to creep up on me. My friends appeared to be finding it; they were settling down. I had been going from one boyfriend to the next; I was having fun – or so I thought. Young, free and single. It all started to become boring. I started to feel an urgency, an urgency to find the thing with no name.

I thought marriage would be the answer, in a town when to be past twenty and not have either a ring on your finger or a baby in a pram meant you were seen as being left on the shelf.

Once again I was considering others' ideals as the way to live my life. It was the 'norm' once more.

Time was getting on, or so I thought. I was the ripe old age of eighteen, and I knew I would have to change soon if I was to be what was expected of me. It was time to settle down. The things I had once given priority to no longer seemed important. Panic began to set in. I had begun to feel lost amongst all my happy married friends – they weren't interested in my latest conquest; the only things they appeared to be interested in were the price of mince and what they would have for that night's tea. The thing that scared the shit out of me was how attractive this seemed to me.

When I met my husband I thought he was all I'd ever hoped and wished for. As my mum said, 'We learn from our mistakes'. This was to be one of my biggest ones. I thought I was in love – whatever that means. He was a good worker, secure and dependable. 'You're so lucky,' I was told by my family and friends. I know now that the love you feel at nineteen is different from the love you experience after seven long years of marriage. It changed from one of romance and chocolates to a love of routine and obligation.

I wanted the full works: a wedding with all the trimmings. I wanted it to be the same as all my friends'. Although religion has never meant much to me, I still wanted the church, the white dress and the photos (to look back on in our old age). Little did I know it was to take more than these things to make a marriage and make it work. Maybe I should have followed my gut feeling as I put that dress on – to run as far and as fast as I could. But it was part of the big plan I had made for myself. I had made my bed and I was going to lie in it. Again failure was my biggest fear – well, maybe not so much the feeling it would give me but the image it would give to those who surrounded me.

There I was, I had become a product of Thatcher's Britain. I had the good husband, the house, the twenty-five-year mortgage and all the trappings of what it took to be acceptable and respected. I had been converted and had never realised, I had become something, someone that I couldn't and didn't like very much. The much-wanted normality had now arrived, and I was stuck with it. I was sure things would get better – they had to, as this was now real life and not a game. I became unbelievably selfish. What did I care if there were three million on the dole, or that people were homeless because of the new social security rules? It all meant nothing to me; I had caught the 'I'm all right Jack' syndrome.

Here I was, the girl who had once joined a union and been willing to strike if it meant better pay for us all. The girl who once would have voiced her opinions so loudly that all who heard would know, who believed in the rights and wrongs of specific political issues, and lived by what she said.

But no more. I had became more interested in whether the mortgage rate was staying low or if we could afford to take a holiday. I'd conformed to all that I had once striven against. I hate to admit it now, but my selfish needs came first, and my politics and beliefs had started to come a very poor second. I'd become a nasty shade of blue. I wanted to be respectable and if that meant living a lie, then I was willing to do it.

Money and security went hand in hand as far as I was concerned. I know now that I was wrong, and I can admit it.

I was prostituting myself, both my mind and my body, for an ideal handed to me by my presumed betters. Surely there was something else – I still hadn't found what I had been looking for; it hadn't appeared with a magic wand after the wedding or since. I wanted something to make it all complete. It dawned on me that the one thing most of my friends had that I didn't was a baby. Anyway, I was being told that it was about time, and I should be getting on with it.

I thought it would be the ultimate experience, the experience of motherhood. I never did and still don't like babies very much, but I knew one of my own would be different. I held this image that after nine months of blissful pregnancy I would give birth (a natural birth) and melt into maternal oblivion. In reality, as before, things didn't work out the way I had imagined.

Those were the most uncomfortable nine months of my life to date. I had none of the wonderful fulfilling feelings promised to me from the pages of those mother-and-baby magazines. Of course at the time I couldn't see that for them to be able to sell those magazines they had to make pregnancy seem like a rewarding experience, otherwise who would buy the bloody things?

Even when the actual giving birth came round I was still influenced by others, but once the pain took over there was only one person who knew what was actually happening to my body, and that was me. Forget the natural birth – whose idea was that anyway? – and give me as much pethidine as possible. All I really knew was that I had never in all my life experienced anything like it, and I knew then that I would probably never do it again. Another myth down the drain. I was beginning to see that the thing I had been searching for would never be found through other people; it could only be found within myself.

I now had a son. I held him near to me, and waited for the feelings to flow – they didn't come. Well, not then, at least.

Once at home with my baby, my husband and all the associated trappings of a successful family, I began to settle back into the routine I'd made for myself before the arrival of my new role in life . . . Only the baby made times for myself few and far between; I'd condemned myself to a life of nappies and feeding times. Years of limbo were to follow. I was told I was having a dose of the baby blues, and things would return to normal soon. Looking back, I think I was even quite good at the housework bit. I took my stand, though, at having the tea ready on the table. I tried to get my husband to share the load, but people told me it was wrong of me to expect a man who had been out working all day to come home and have to make his own meals and get the baby ready for bed. Here I was once more being the selfish bitch I'd always been. It was a no-win situation.

By this time interest rates were low and it encouraged my husband and me to borrow and to buy a nice car, sell our home and move into the idyllic cottage we are told is every girl's dream. It was the beginning of the end for my marriage. It had it all: the little bit of garden that is so prized as a status symbol and the chickens at the end of the garden. The good life – or so I thought.

During this time the relationship between my husband and me changed; it was no longer the wine-and-roses we'd experienced before the birth of our son. There was no time to spend on building it; all the time was spent on fixing the house up, looking after Daniel and my husband working all the hours possible in order to pay for this good life. I had thought things were good, but in reality the only things that had happened were in order to have these nice possessions; our feelings and emotions were put on stand-by while we paid these low interest loans. Nothing mattered apart from keeping our heads above water and our image of the successful marriage. It became a sham, both in public and in private. Our sex life stopped and I was glad it stopped. I no longer felt happy; all I felt was tired and wanting to be left alone.

At one point I thought there was something medically wrong. Here I was six years married and I couldn't stand the thought of my husband near me, although I still cared for him to a certain extent. So off I went to the family doctor with high hopes of some miracle cure, some pill to make it all better. I had not been prepared for what he was to say to me. I had tried to explain to him, but much to my horror he looked over his glasses at me and frowned: 'But he's your husband, Mrs Nichol; he has his rights; just lie back and think of Scotland – the more you have it the more you'll want it.' I couldn't believe my ears. I'd gone to this man and bared not only my soul but my body, and he'd thrown me out of his office with a remark like that. I was slowly beginning to realise that he had spoken to me maybe not with the attitude of a doctor but with the attitude of a man. I was not naive enough to base my judgement of men on this one man's insensitivity, but it had become clear through the past years of marriage that it was an attitude my husband also appeared to accept.

I think he was becoming bored with my petty feminine problems. I felt imprisoned in my own home and by my husband and child. After my encounter with my doctor I started to question more what right he had to say that to me – I questioned not only his attitude but the way I was being treated in general: I was somebody's wife, somebody's mum, but never me; I was becoming a nonentity and I was terrified. I was becoming lost. I could see no way out of my situation; the only thing I knew was I had to survive – or escape somehow.

Things became a little better as my son got older and I had a bit more time to do the things I had once enjoyed, reading and writing poetry. It gave me time to breathe and to forget about the worry of rising interest rates. It's strange that the rise and fall of my marriage seemed to coincide with the economic climate.

I even escaped occasionally from my prison and travelled

out into the big wide world, outside those hills. I went to London to stay with a friend. I had never encountered anything like it. Here was a world outside mine; people were living and breathing and doing something more with their lives than the bare existence I had been experiencing. I would return home with my strength renewed until the next time I could raise enough money (stolen from my housekeeping) and go once again into that big wide world.

I think my husband thought that allowing me this freedom would keep me from doing anything drastic. I think he knew that one day it would not be enough.

I looked for something (once again) to stretch my mind, as my grey cells were starting to revive for the first time in years – in a direction that surprised me, and my family. I wanted to have some sort of education; I strove for books and knowledge. My mum couldn't understand; she kept asking 'Why now?' I'd had my chance at school, now was the time for getting on with my family. Nevertheless I was determined to do something. This time it was all my decision, there was no one looking over my shoulder telling me I was right or wrong. I felt alive. I began to feel a fire inside me and I think my husband could see it burning. He stood back and watched me. To give him credit, he knew he was losing me, but still he helped me find time to do the things I was interested in – maybe his was a real love.

I started an Open University course in, of all things, Women's Studies – it was the fatal blow; it only confirmed the feminist views that I had gradually begun to feel comfortable with. My shades of blue had subsided with the lack of importance I had begun to give to what people thought of me. I could admit that I had made mistakes and that I had betrayed myself over the past years, but I think to admit them can go some way to rectifying them. I had made them trying to fulfil other people's expectations, but now I was only going to try to deal with one person's expectations – of course money was important, but I no longer felt happy about selling my soul for it; I was starting to feel some sort of self-worth. I am important both as woman and as person. Maybe I had failed, but if this meant admitting my failure as a wife, then so be it; I knew I couldn't fail at being a woman, as it was the one thing I was certain of.

I returned from a week away from home; I had made a decision, and that was to leave. I told my husband, and to my surprise he agreed that things weren't working and we had both changed. It was a relief to me that he made it as easy as he could. Our son was to be the biggest consideration; he hadn't asked to be born, he had been part of the big plan. So why should he suffer because of my wish for experience? I would take him and try to manage as best I could – try not to make the same mistakes that I had made proving myself to others.

I know that the decisions made in the last year of the eighties have taken me into the nineties maybe not a better person but a wiser one. I have developed from a naive and silly teenager into a woman whom I know, like and feel comfortable being.

I have left the town that would have liked to keep me in my place, and left a political way of thinking that considers money more important than people, especially women. I'm no longer going to conform to the norm; I'm going to be the person I want to be. If that means having little money and no permanent home and being laughed at for my politics, so be it.

The past ten years have been lived by other people's standards. I'm going to live the next ten, if I'm strong enough to do so, by my own. I feel as if I've been waging a war, and I'm now emerging with a strength built up from all my negative experiences. I have begun to turn them into positive ones.

At least I have been able to find the courage to make the changes in my life. The only regret I have is that the friends and family I have left behind, who have maybe felt some of the anxieties I have had, never will have or never had the strength to go with their instincts.

I now feel able to love my son, as I can see that to love him I first had to like myself and know myself, then show my true feelings, not just what I've been expected to feel.

As I've said, I'm looking back from where I've run to; I've come full circle from depending on the state, to a middle-class existence, to once again having money passed to me over the post office counter. But I can live with it, I'm now my woman, my own woman, as far as I can manage to be.

I know now that security and low interest rates can't make my life easy. Maybe I have failed others' expectations of me, but what the hell; I'm at the point where I don't really care. Daniel and I are the main actors in this play, and I'm going to act for all I'm worth.

I can live hand in hand with my politics and feel good about it; I'm no longer in conflict with my conscience.

I just hope that the next girl who puts on one of those white dresses finds the courage to run if that's what she feels like doing. Then again, maybe she will be able to take that experience as I have done and use it to make herself a woman she will come to know and like.

6

Us Over Here –
Them Over There

Jacqueline McCafferty

We've got a unique little situation over here in Northern
Ireland. Not only do we have to put up with Thatcher's
economic policies, but we have to put up with her Northern
Ireland political policy as well. The British think they're
badly off under her. They should take a trip over here and see
the mess she's made.

I must admit I've come through the Thatcher regime relatively unscathed so far – a few minor scratches here and
there, that's all. Nothing to worry about though, considering
that not only am I from a Catholic, working-class background,
I've also been raised by my mother since she and my father
separated when I was six years old. I would say I'm one of
the exceptions to the theory that children from single-parent,
working-class families tend to be underachievers. We weren't
particularly well off, but so far I've achieved everything I set
out to. I wish that lots of others could say the same thing.

So – what's she done to us in the past ten years? From a
Catholic viewpoint nothing dramatically different from her
predecessors between 1190 and 1979. The bloodshed, the
violence, the poverty, the unemployment, continue as
normal. From the Protestant side, maybe they're a bit worried

that she's about to sell them out. I know their belts are tightening as the economy slides further down. Even east of the Bann poverty is hitting hard.

My childhood was spent in the Bogside in Derry during the height of the present conflict. For me the sound of gunfire, explosions, the smell of tear gas and the sight of armed men, tanks and Saracens wasn't extraordinary; it was life. I didn't understand what was happening. I was told the soldiers were our enemies and that we Catholics were fighting the British and the Prods because they were bad to us.

My mother wasn't a very political person, so at home politics were never talked about. My brother and I weren't allowed to read newspapers because they contained too much 'sex and scandal', so I grew up unaware of many things except the violence on my front doorstep. Even in this respect I was naive, since at the first sign of a battle my mother ushered me off the street into the house until everything had calmed down, leaving my friends to throw bricks at the army, and the youths to lob any kind of bomb they could get their hands on. This happened quite frequently in the early '70s and my mother was pleased at her efforts to keep my mind and thoughts free from republican contamination. However, she didn't know about the Saturday afternoons I spent in my aunt's hairdressing salon on the edge of the battlefield watching (along with my very Republican aunts and grandmother) the fight between people and army rage on. Nor did she know about the conversations I heard in my grandmother's house at dinner time each school day. The house was always crowded with influential people talking about politics. I was too young to understand everything, but old enough to be influenced by what I heard and saw.

At the age of eleven I went to the local convent grammar school, where I was told my goals in life – to do my O and A levels, go on to university and, most importantly, to be a good Christian, wife and mother. In that year we also moved to a big council housing estate on the outskirts of Derry. The houses were built as part of the government's package of reforms for Northern Ireland. It was an attempt to appease the Catholics who, for a long time, had been discriminated against as far as housing allocation was concerned. It was nice, very quiet, with lots of green fields and open spaces and lots of children and married couples. I was very happy with life. Only later did it come to my attention that the layout of these estates was also a deliberate security policy – with only one entrance and exit, enabling the army and police to confine trouble to a small area. They also broke up the tightly knit nationalist communities of the Creggan and Bogside.

I was vaguely aware of Labour, Liberals, the Tories, from my history lessons and from the news, but all that was far removed from me. My friends and I were more interested in boyfriends and discos, dates and Youth Clubs than politics. Anyway, the politicians were all over there across the water, making rules and regulations in London, and things like benefits, unemployment, homelessness and income tax had no relevance in my life at that time. So how the hell was I supposed to know who Margaret Thatcher was? She just arrived on the scene one day, and she's been here ever since.

I remember the 1979 election results quite clearly. I was with my friends on the school bus casually commenting on the election: 'Britain has a new Prime Minister, she's a woman!' At that time she was still 'over there' and we were over here. We couldn't vote, and even if we could our choices weren't Labour, Liberal or Conservative. They were the Social Democratic and Labour Party (SDLP), the Democratic Unionist Party (DUP) and the Official Unionist Party (OUP). So what possible relevance could it have for us? She felt the same way about us: who the hell are they? She hardly knew of our existence until two bombs killed Mountbatten and eighteen soldiers at Warrenpoint in August 1979 and she paid her first visit here to offer sympathy and boost army morale (heaven help them!).

The first major issue under Thatcher was the 1980 hunger

strike by Republican prisoners in Long Kesh. It only lasted a short time, no one died, no one gained anything. Then came the second one, the big one, in 1981. Ten men dead, murdered by her officiating from over there. All they wanted was to be granted political status. Wasn't it fitting in a war situation to be called a prisoner of war? She refused to move. We waited and listened: daily reports; men were getting weaker; losing their sight; losing the use of their limbs; lying in prison hospitals; fading away. I didn't believe she'd let them die. I thought the news would come – the hunger strike is over, the prisoners have won. It didn't. At 2 a.m. on 5 May 1981 I heard the motor cavalcade proclaim the news to Derry city: Bobby Sands was dead, and I prayed with all my Catholic heart for him.

I'd never heard of the man until he went on hunger strike, but I felt a sense of loss at his death and bitterness at her. Why did she let it go so far? Day by day she heard reports; she could have prevented it, but she didn't. She let him and nine others die, insisting: 'I will not give in to terrorists'. I was in my second year of Thatcherism and I was beginning to realise that although I'd never been to London, it wasn't as far away as I'd previously imagined.

From September 1981 to June 1983 I was busy at school studying for my A levels and things were pretty quiet on the home front except for the occasional riot, bomb, and murder. However, in Britain in 1983 all hell was breaking loose with election fever and the Falklands War. I didn't much care about what was happening over there. It was an English, not an Irish, problem and as I was still at school and dependent on my mother, who fortunately had a job, I wasn't really affected by the economics of Thatcher though I knew she was a hard woman, with no time or sympathy for the 'idlers' and the 'not-so-well-off'. All I heard on the news was how the rich were being rewarded for having money and the poor were being penalised for having none. My granny would moan about her old age pension and how she (Thatcher) was 'robbing us blind'. 'You old hypocrite', my family would mutter whenever her face appeared on television. When she won the election again there was an uproar: 'Saints and Jesus preserve us all, another four years of her!' we all chorused.

In the meantime I was having multiple nervous breakdowns over my A levels, wondering if I would pass. Would I go to Manchester or Liverpool university? I was in Greece when the results came out: I'd passed, and I celebrated with a bottle of ouzo. However, I didn't get high enough grades for the universities of my choice, so I went to Sunderland Polytechnic. I was petrified leaving home, living away from 'mummy' for the first time in my life. I cried the whole way from Derry to Sunderland, and continued crying for two weeks.

My arrival in Sunderland was a bit of a shock. It was cold, bleak, grey and about as economically depressed as Derry – definitely an anti-Thatcher haven. I couldn't understand the strong north-east accent and they couldn't understand my broad Derry drawl, so communication was a nightmare. The only thought on my mind was 'When's the next plane to Belfast?' To make matters worse, the halls of residence were full so I was dumped in lodgings across the river, miles from anywhere, no friends and no one to talk to except the family I lodged with. I knew I couldn't stay there, I would have gone crazy.

Things worked out okay. After a week of just me and 'the family' another student moved in. She was a big, tough, intimidating Jewish woman from London. She was anti-Thatcher, pro-Palestine (much to the horror of her parents), feminist, and I was terrified of her. She thought I was a nice little girly type but after getting pissed together at a birthday party we discovered that we liked each other and got on well together so we decided to find a flat. Goodbye family, hello real student life.

Student life was both exciting and frightening. Going to lectures, spending my meagre grant (at least I got a grant, I suppose I should be thankful) in the student bar, meeting new friends, people from all walks of life: punks, hippies, trendies, upper classes and middle classes. There weren't so many of my class, the good old working class. Conversations revolved around what was 'ideologically sound or unsound': Thatcher, Kinnock, revolutionary communism (what?), vegetarianism, feminism, ageism, racism, sexism. I was lost in all these 'isms'. I was quite popular among all these mad radicals (or as I called them, 'mad rads') because I was a Northern Irish Catholic and it was 'really cool and ideologically sound and rad' to support British withdrawal and Irish independence.

Sometimes I found this attitude quite annoying. I listened to these people spouting off about Northern Ireland without really being aware of what exactly was going on over here. You can know a lot about something but you can't understand what it feels like unless you have experienced it first hand, and as none of these upper- and middle-class 'rads' had been to Ireland before, they had no idea what it was like to live with war and poverty in a working-class area.

Derry has, and always has had, a high, long-term unemployment rate. Youngsters leave school at sixteen and are still unemployed at twenty. Parents are better off on the dole because wage levels are so low. Emigration for many is a fact of life; the young people head off to the golden streets of London in search of work and the educated mostly choose not to come back. Why spend three years at university to come home to a £90-a-week job (if you're lucky)?

While Thatcher was busy talking of new ventures, industrial growth and economic advancement, it seemed that we'd been forgotten about. We were still going downhill. Factories closed, no one wanted to invest money here. Why should they? Why bring industry to a place where tomorrow war could destroy it? Maybe it's also got something to do with the fact that Derry is two-thirds Catholic. Discrimination is rife here; it was the main grievance put forward by the Civil Rights Movement in 1969. I quickly enlightened these 'rads' and let them know that it wasn't just a war of religions but also a war of economics.

I once had to make a speech on the subject at the students' representative council. It was during the implementation of the Anglo-Irish Agreement. An Irish Protestant – sorry, I should say an Ulster Protestant member of the Conservative Society – wanted our student union to write a letter of support for Thatcher. I was coerced by my 'mad rad' friends into making a speech opposing the motion (me a public speaker! I still tremble when I think of it). I agreed only if I could bolster myself up first in the bar.

The Protestant guy made his speech about majorities, Protestant interests, UK citizenship, blah, blah, blah. It was quite a boring, unemotional speech and only the handful of Tory supporters clapped when he finished. Then, shaking and breathless, I stood up. My friends were all behind me: 'Go on Jack, go for it.' I launched into my spiel about imperialism, discrimination, harassment, poverty, unemployment, and second-class citizenship. I brought the house down and the 'mad rads' went crazy. The Tories were defeated and I, still shaking, was taken to the bar and pumped full of alcohol to calm me down.

I had adapted quite well to student life and got on well with a lot of people, apart from the rugby club members, who could always be seen in the bar, downing their pints, singing raunchy songs and slagging off women – obnoxious gits. My friends and I used to have regular run-ins with them and they detested us: 'Fuck off, you bra-burning feminists. Why don't you go and have a real screw with a man?' Obviously all this pissing around on the rugby field knocked out of their heads any intelligence they might have had in the first place.

I also wasn't very popular with the Tories, for obvious reasons. I'd had their motion defeated and my circle of friends consisted of 'mad rads', a Tory nightmare. Just after the Brighton bombing in 1984, they could be seen, ashen-faced and sombre. I think they were having a period of mourning – after all, their mighty leader had just escaped a horrific death. I wonder what would have happened had she been killed? There'd probably have been a purge, a 'Send the Irish back to Ireland' campaign. A few of my Derry friends at other colleges in England encountered some hostility after the bomb. It wasn't anything serious, just insulting comments like 'Irish bastard' or 'IRA bastard, crawl back to where you came from'. I had people coming to me offering their commiserations. 'For what?' I'd say. Their reply – 'Better luck next time'. But to tell the truth, I thought it was a pretty stupid move by the Provos. What would they have achieved? Nothing, except martyrdom for her. Can you imagine it? 'Maggie the martyr' and some equally frozen-faced Tory to take her place. No thank you!

I spent three years in Sunderland. It wasn't the most inspiring or beautiful place, but I enjoyed it, and after getting to grips with the north-east accent I found the people were akin to the Irish, with little trace of the 'stiff upper lip' reserve that you often associate with the English. During these years I learned a hell of a lot about Thatcher. Everywhere there was evidence of her reign. I could see what she was doing to others around me: to the majority of workers and low-income taxpayers, those dependent on welfare benefits, the miners in 1984.

The grant she gave me wasn't very substantial, but have students ever had enough to live on? They usually leave college with an overdraft. I got around £1600 to pay for everything. I didn't go hungry or anything, but my house was pretty cold because I couldn't afford to heat it properly. Sunderland winters are really severe. Taking a bath in ten inches of lukewarm water was no joke, and dressing and going to bed was usually done under my two duvets.

At Christmas, Easter and summer, I had to hitch home as the fare was £40 return and my travel allowance was £50 a year. I left college with an overdraft, but as I said, I was lucky to get a grant. What's going to happen when the loan system comes into effect? The next priority after graduating will be to find a job to pay off this massive debt. I was lucky. I had a choice: work, further study or travel.

I opted for travel. It was something I'd always wanted to do, to see Asia. Someone had mentioned to me and my boyfriend that you could earn upwards of $1000 a week working in fish factories in Alaska. It sounded much better than a boring job in London. The plan was to travel in India and Nepal for a while, then head for Japan to teach English. Off we went to Alaska to earn the funds for the trip. We left London with the air fare to Canada and £100 in our pockets, and hitchhiked from Toronto to Anchorage. For the next three months we lived in tent cities, sometimes working twenty hours a day gutting salmon.

During my time there I met lots of people. Some of the Americans were quite nice and could say the word 'communism' without flinching, but I found a lot of them to be extreme in their views. Many nights were spent round the campfire, drinking beer and having arguments. I remember one night in particular, when tempers and nerves were raw because of lack of sleep. There were six Mexicans (one of whom was a distant relative of Fidel Castro), one Scot (my boyfriend) and me, against an army of commie-hating, democracy-loving Americans. The argument covered freedom of choice in the USA, capitalism, Reagan, Thatcher, communism, and terrorism – me making the main contribution here. They thought the struggle for Irish independence was wonderful, this being the only point during the whole argument that we agreed on. Then they went on to Gaddafi. America had bombed Libya only a few days before and the Yanks were celebrating: 'Good old Ronnie, wonderful Thatcher, she let the planes leave from England, kill Gaddafi, the fucking terrorist, death to all terrorists.' Well, correct me if I'm wrong, but I always thought the IRA were classed as terrorists, a fact I pointed out to the Americans. 'Doesn't matter,' they replied. 'What you're doing is wunnerful, just wunnerful.' Now – what can you say to that? I couldn't believe them. They loved Reagan, Thatcher, the IRA, their freedom – what freedom, when you're constantly bombarded with anti-commie, pro-capitalist propaganda? There's no choice in America, you're either capitalist or you're nothing. At least over here we do have the opportunity to choose.

We made quite a lot of money in Alaska but it didn't stretch far enough for our travel plans, and on arriving home I discovered that I'd spent about two-thirds of what I'd earned. Sob! Not enough money for India.

I spent the next four months in Derry, on the dole, miserable, bored and skint. During the week I watched television and went out on Friday or Saturday for a drink. By March 1987 I'd had enough. I was still thinking about India, but there was no way I'd get a job in Derry to raise the necessary funds. So once again I packed my bags and took off, like so many other young Irish folk, to the bright lights of London, to seek my fortune.

For the first month I lived with a friend, the anti-Thatcher, pro-Palestine feminist from college, at her parents' house. What a house! It was in East Finchley (Thatcher's constituency) in a very exclusive road. King Fahd of Saudi Arabia actually had a mansion in that road. My friend's house was huge. It had an indoor swimming pool, jacuzzi, three bathrooms, three cars, all mod cons and a gardener and domestic. They didn't have a drinks cupboard, they had a drinks shed, piled full of bottles of expensive cognac, and to top it all, her parents were in America for a month so it was no trouble for me to stay. I'd never experienced such wealth before, and coming from a typical three-bedroom council house, I felt out of my depth sometimes.

I got a shitty job handing out leaflets in the street. Each evening when I came home, I had a refreshing swim in the pool and then dinner with a bottle of cognac. It was sheer bliss. However, it didn't last long. Her mother came home and she didn't have much time for this Irish working-class twit. She made me feel unpolished and uncouth and I felt it was time to find my own place. Oh well! It was nice while it lasted.

I moved into a house quite near my friend's place and carried on handing out leaflets and freezing and being snubbed on the streets of London. I thought to hell with this, so I signed on at an employment agency which eventually found me a temporary job in a bank in the heart of the financial area. God, I hated the place! It was full of yuppies and middle-aged, middle-class men, being extremely polite to me – 'After you, my dear'; holding doors open for me, saying 'Thank you' in soft patronising tones and stamping me into the ground after work in their rush to get on the tube.

As I said, it was 1987: election year once again. I even saw Thatcher during her campaigning. She was visiting East Finchley to woo her supporters. I didn't intentionally go to see her. I just happened to see a crowd in the street one day, and being a naturally nosy person, I went over to investigate. There she was in the flesh, and I can tell you I was in a bad mood for the rest of the day. There were a lot of people cheering for her. A few pensioners were standing beside me and one shouted, 'Good for you, Maggie, we're behind you all the way', and I muttered to myself, 'You'll not be saying that next month when your pensions are cut and inflation goes up!'

On the night of the election I arrived home at 11 p.m. The results were coming in from Scotland and the North of England: 'Victory for Labour', 'Labour topples Tories'. I was really excited. I thought, 'Maybe Labour does have a chance'. But next morning it was all over. I heard the news: 'Maggie's done it again', and Britain was divided into North and South.

Shortly after this my jobs ended and again my only income was the dole. I spent the rest of the summer between London, Scotland and Ireland, because it's impossible to find work in London during this period. In September I got another temporary job in a bank and my 'mad rad' friends will never let me forget this episode. What did I do? I did the boring administration work for Rolls-Royce and the TSB during their privatisation. I didn't particularly enjoy handling cheques for £2 million from company ABC or the Right Honourable Blah, but I was due to leave for India at the end of October and I desperately needed cash. What do you think of that? I threw my principles to the wind for £700.

The exit from Britain was quite dramatic. Our bags packed, due to leave the next day, my boyfriend, some friends and I headed off to the pub for a farewell piss-up and on the way home we were commenting on how windy it was. In the morning we woke to the news: 'This is an emergency, do not leave your homes unless it is absolutely necessary.' The South had been hit by a 'hurricane'. Well, emergency or no emergency, we had to hitchhike to Athens to catch our flight to Bombay, so in the midst of the debris and destruction we said goodbye to Britain for what were to be two incredible years in Asia.

We spent our first six months in India and Nepal and I learned a few things about materialism. I didn't feel particularly wealthy, but to the Indians I was filthy rich. I could come to their country, travel, stay in hotels for six months. One thing I discovered on my travels was that the further East I went, the more Thatcher was admired. Many Indians have a great respect for her. I don't know why – she's really messed them around when it comes to immigration.

After India we spent a year teaching English in Taiwan, having given up our plan of going to Japan owing to lack of funds. That year passed very quickly, and in February 1989 I decided it was time to pack up and start my return journey to the West. This time I was alone.

One of the first places I stopped off at was Hong Kong. There's a lot of wealth there, but the Hong Kong Chinese are worried about what will happen in 1997 when it's handed back to the People's Republic. When I was there in March 1989 there were huge anti-Thatcher demonstrations. It's hardly surprising that people are worried, particularly after what happened in Tiananmen Square.

Several months later, via Thailand, India and Nepal, I arrived back in Britain. It was a bigger culture shock than arriving in India for the first time. It took me two hours to pluck up enough courage to leave the airport and get on a tube. I was almost skint and needed to get back to Ireland quickly because I'd picked up hepatitis two weeks before. I got the first boat home. Arriving in Derry was extremely strange. The longest I'd ever been away before was seven months. I felt like a tourist. I saw many things I hadn't noticed before: little details on buildings and streets, expressions on people's faces, things I'd always taken for granted.

The Provos had arranged a welcome-home gala for me. As I came into the city I heard a bomb go off, then lots of smoke and police and army Land Rovers screaming all over the place. Both bridges across the river to the Catholic side were sealed off and I couldn't get home. So – the IRA and the army are still at it. Unionists and Nationalists are still niggling about the Anglo-Irish Agreement, Free Ireland and no surrender. And the latest thing is that Sinn Fein can't talk on television any more.

It took me a while to get used to being in the Western world once again; to fit back into the city I hadn't seen for so long.

On the surface there seemed to be a change for the better. Derry looked good: new buildings, shops, roads, trees, and people appeared to have more to do. There was more consciousness of important issues: the environment, apartheid, homosexuality, AIDS; lots of new groups had been established, resource centres, unemployment centres, job clubs, law centres – but underneath the surface things weren't good at all. Sixteen- and seventeen-year-olds on the Youth Training Programme (YTP); jobs advertised were all part-time, one year Action for Community Employment (ACE) low-paid jobs (clever little trick by Thatcher to reduce the unemployment figures). Poverty is even more rampant as people's benefits don't rise with inflation and the dole 'lends' money for essential items. People who were unemployed when I left are still unemployed. People wait for their giros so they can go out at the weekend to get pissed, while the rest of the week is spent watching television until 4 a.m. getting up at 1 p.m. and going out to 'actively seek work'. The big council estate which was once nice today stinks of decay and deprivation.

One day, by chance, I called in to the Job Centre just to look at what was available and I noticed a part-time ACE job as a welfare rights researcher for £60 a week. It sounded interesting, so I applied and got the job. I've been doing it for some months now and I quite like it. Pity about the money, though. The ironic thing is that the job was advertised wrongly; it should have read 'unemployment researcher', which is my official title. It's taking me a year to research what I already knew: there are no jobs in Derry and unemployment rates are still among the highest in the UK. People laugh at me when I tell them what I do. We in Derry have a terrific sense of humour. You have to laugh or you'd cry.

So what do I see for the future? Not much if Maggie keeps getting her way. I don't think she will, though. Come the next election, she'll be out. But are Labour any more capable of building our depressed and divided city? I don't think so. Britain is clinging to the remains of its colonial empire and hampering our growth in the process. Give us our freedom, Britain, so we can build our socialist republic; the days of your mighty empire are over.

Postscript

The day after I finished this piece, three Socialist Republicans (i.e. the IRA) entered my house and held me and my mother hostage for three hours. They were masked and armed, and demanded the keys to our car. My mother flatly refused so they got quite aggressive, claiming that they were under orders to use the car for a military operation and wouldn't take no for an answer. I had a gun put to my face when I refused to believe they were IRA and their guns were real. My mother got very angry, however, and a heated argument ensued. Eventually they backed down and said they would call a taxi and hijack it instead, but we were to remain hostages until the operation had been carried out. The reason for this change of plan was probably the fact that there was no man in the house. They couldn't harm two women without drawing bad publicity, especially as it was only five days after the Bloody Sunday commemoration march which went drastically wrong, with a bomb killing a sixteen-year-old boy instead of the security forces. At 5 p.m. they said they were leaving; the operation had been called off. They ordered us not to move for at least ten minutes to enable them to make their escape.

Ten minutes later I phoned the police. They refused to come out and said that we had to go to them. My mother said, 'We have had a very traumatic experience. If you want to talk to us come to our house.' Again they said, 'No, come tomorrow at three o'clock.' After thinking it over we decided to go and have it finished with. The police gave me a harder time than the IRA. After they had kept us waiting for thirty minutes my mother was taken by one detective to a fingerprint room. I was taken by two men down dark corridors past lots of closed doors, doors which led into interrogation rooms. I was taken into one such room. It contained three chairs, one table, and a camera which was focused on me for two and half hours. I knew what they were trying to do: trying to find some connection between me and the IRA. What made us change our minds about coming to the station? Did I know the guys? (Insinuating that I had invited them into my house.) Were the guns long-shooters or short-shooters? How did I know? To me one looked like a cowboy gun, the other like a potato-gun. One guy questioned me constantly; the other kept silent. The IRA men had a plastic bag which contained something that looked like a video cassette case; did I see it?

What did I think it was? Was it a bomb? When they discovered that I worked in the Bogside they gave each other knowing glances: she must be one of them if she works there.

I found out later that my mother had commented to her detective on police bias, the assumption that just because you're a Catholic you know something. The guy agreed that this attitude was prevalent among the RUC. You're automatically thought to be involved because of your religion. After one and a half hours of questioning, my statement was taken: eight pages of writing. I was beginning to get impatient and indignant. I had done my duty in reporting the incident, and the police were keeping me almost as long as the IRA had. My thoughts went to the numerous people who'd been detained there. I hadn't been arrested. Those who had could be held for seven days without being charged.

Sure I was angry at the IRA for putting me through that ordeal. They've left me nervous and paranoid, but in a way I can understand their reasoning – after all, they were from my side of the divide. But to our 'protectors', the Royal Ulster Constabulary, my mother and I were just another two Fenians, and by their behaviour and suspicious attitude they left me feeling as if I'd contrived the whole situation. Is it any wonder Catholics have little faith in the so-called security forces?

7
Pride and Protest

Jayne Kelly

I was fifteen at the start of the eighties. I can't remember New Year. I was probably trying to avoid one of my mother's parties by babysitting.

I took my O levels and went on to the sixth form at the same school. I stayed on at school because everyone did (in that area, anyway, which was a sort of aspiring middle-class housing estate where everyone had a similar house apart from the added extensions). Also I didn't feel old enough to leave school. As regards the world, I knew barely nothing at all. My dad insisted on buying only the *Yorkshire Post* because he liked the crossword and he was a Yorkshire MAN. I occasionally glanced at the headlines or the TV pages.

I can remember crying a lot and writing bad, passionate poems about being an outcast from society, because by then I had decided that I was a lesbian and my life would be orientated around women. I found this confusing as I knew no other women like me, and frightening as I knew a lot of people would hate me, particularly my parents. So I pushed them a long way from me emotionally so that it wouldn't matter if they rejected me. It tended to make me feel worse rather than better.

Occasionally I would read *Spare Rib* or *Sanity*, which would appear at school, and that's all my political education consisted of – except that I read hundreds of books which, along with my progressive school, formed my views to be a million miles away from my parents'. They're Conservative supporters, racist, think Margaret Thatcher is wonderful for getting the country back into shape. I believed in Labour or no political party, anti-racism, and I disliked Thatcher.

I got terrible A level results because of my total imcomprehension of physics. I couldn't go to the university I'd chosen, so instead I went to a polytechnic in Lancashire. There I shared a house with four other women. One of them none of us liked much; she used to have a theory a week about why I was a pervert. One of the others couldn't understand me at all but thought I was fun to go out with. The other two were Welsh: one very nice, the other very straight-minded, but she supported me, particularly during hangovers.

At the student union I learnt about anti-apartheid, how lousy Tory policies were, and the miners' strike.

The father of one of the Welsh women was a miner so we watched the news a lot and collected money and organised pickets at the college. I went home for a visit during this period. Even my parents were talking about it. My mother said she wouldn't let a miner into her house even if he were starving. I stormed out, feeling very angry about how little she knew and how prejudiced she was.

Eventually I told her one night: I was a lesbian. Three phrases she said stick in my memory: 'I wish you'd never been born', 'Don't tell your father', and 'Are you the man or the woman?' I ignored the first, told her she had a month to tell Dad, and went into a lengthy discussion about equality and sharing in response to the third. As I left to go back to college she called out, 'Remember you're a girl'. She didn't speak of it again for years.

To try and meet some women like me I went to a gay switchboard meeting. Most of the women there were huge, violent and paranoid about discovery. I kept going because there wasn't anything else. But I questioned whether I'd made the right decision, as a lot of the men at college were nicer and gentler.

Because I was miserable and there was a sweet shop two doors down, I put on two and a half stone. I got into a mess with one of the switchboard women; this taught me that being a lesbian doesn't necessarily mean you are committed to women, sharing or equality. I was, they weren't. I started smoking and lost the extra weight in about a month.

Somewhere in the middle of this I met some women at college who had been to Greenham Common Peace Camp. They said it was wonderful: lots of music, mud, tents and lesbians who were feminists. I kept thinking I would go one day. I got more and more bored with the degree course I was doing. It felt as if I'd been taking exams for years and years. I couldn't concentrate on my revising, so instead I decided to go and see Greenham for myself. I knew it was below Oxford and had a home-drawn map from Newbury.

I set off at about 5 a.m. The coach was cancelled so I got one at 8 a.m. instead. I got on, but it kept making stops and people with suitcases and silly hats got on. Finally, after three rounds of 'Viva l'España', I asked someone if it was the right coach to Oxford. She looked at me as if I was an idiot and said No, it was an excursion to Benidorm! I hurtled downstairs and stopped the coach. Finally I got to Newbury, misread the map, and ended up at Greenham at about 8 p.m. It was dark, everyone looked miserable, I shared a tin of sweetcorn with someone and went to bed.

The next day I wandered around the base to the other gates to find that there was an action that afternoon. The women there were planning for around 300 to 600 women to enter the base during one day. You didn't have to answer police questions except to give a name, which could be false, such as Lilli Lett or Tammy Pax; that was all I knew.

I went into the base at 7 p.m. I was arrested and put into a

Portacabin with hundreds of women. I was finally processed, saw the police and had my details taken at 6 a.m. the next morning. I'm 5'5", green eyes, brown hair (well, I had a pink Mohican then). They said I was 5'9", blue eyes, blonde hair. They terrified me; I'd only ever seen the police in the role of the village bobby or the one who does your cycling proficiency and lets you play with his radio. I found them very intimidating, potentially violent and abusive. When I was let out I went round to the gate and stayed a couple of days. Then I went back to college, got a lot more clothes, and left to live permanently at Greenham Common. It was the best thing I'd ever done.

About five weeks later my parents turned up at blue gate. It was most embarrassing; my dad put his arm round me and about five women immediately came over to rescue me because they thought he was a male visitor harassing me. My mum cried all over me because I was living at a horrible place, with horrible women, and I had no hair (I'd shaved it all off the day before they arrived). I was barefoot because I was sunbathing, and she kept wailing about me having no shoes! They finally left as I collapsed into a wreck, to be revived by whacky baccy (dope).

I found out later that three of my college friends had been taken out of their exams to give assurances to her that I hadn't attempted suicide and I wasn't in a hospital dying. Where she got this idea from I don't know, because I had written twice to say I was living at Greenham. Perhaps she thought suicide was the only alternative to Greenham.

I loved living there; I also hated it. I loved living in a community of women; I loved the freedom, learning you could do what you wanted, that no one had to wash up or tidy if they didn't want to (so no one did it); finding women strong, beautiful and wise, who loved the way they wanted and said 'No' to the things they didn't agree with. I hated the cold (but you got used to it), the bailiffs, the squaddies, the missiles. I lived at blue gate, which is the first one the bailiffs visited when they evicted (once or twice a day), so we didn't get any warning about them coming. By the time we'd got our bedding into the van and got the dogs out of the way, they would have taken everything else. Once we had about four or five kittens in an old pram and they threatened to put them in the muncher (a big orange rubbish lorry), turn it on and kill them.

After about a year I went to live in London for a couple of months in a squat in Islington. There I learned about being poor and having no money and about how people with nowhere to live are considered shits by the wealthy. Once a woman friend came to our house after being beaten up by the man she'd married so that she could stay in the country, because she was Spanish. He came to get her, we didn't let him in, so he jumped straight through the window. Two friends grabbed her and ran out of the back door, while he hit me; he was a heroin junkie and completely crazy. He ran out and grabbed the woman, beat her up, while the police we'd called watched. They didn't stop him because he was her husband. We found her a safe house; we had to hide from him as well. After two weeks she went back to him because if she didn't she'd be an illegal immigrant and have to go back to her abusive father.

I grew weary with living in a city and not being involved in anything political, not being involved in any form of action against the male violence that so disempowers us. So I moved back to Greenham again – this time to yellow gate, as I wanted to be more involved with the cruise convoy and it was more political than blue gate.

The anti-nuclear campaign at Greenham wasn't just about cruise missiles. Greenham tried to show women all the connections that male power has formed. The uranium for nuclear warheads comes from poor Black countries where affluent Whites rape the land and defile the sacred places. They test the bombs in the Pacific, where indigenous island-ers are subject to guinea-pig-like conditions. And because the women at Greenham protest and are outside the 'normal' role for women (i.e. not at home) they are subjected to violent physical, sexual and verbal abuse by squaddies, police, American personnel, nearby residents and newspapers, etc. Cruise missiles were just a central focus; all the other issues were there as well, and we protested against them too.

At yellow gate I fell in love with a woman who lived near Greenham; she'd been involved in the camp a lot and also done cruisewatch from the beginning. (Cruisewatchers, along with Greenham women, watch where the convoy goes when it comes out of the base. Then they protest with people, banners, etc., on the route to show that they don't agree with cruise missiles, and to prove that the military idea of cruise being able to melt into the landscape is completely false.)

I moved to live with her and her two boys in a small village about one and a half hours from Greenham. We did a lot of cruisewatching then, and still do, though less often now. We get a phone call, usually from my lover's mother (because she's very involved in cruisewatch as well) to say that the convoy might be coming out tonight. We drive to the convoy's usual route in the middle of the night, 12 or 1 a.m. Then we wait by the side of the road with a banner saying 'Blood on your hands'. Usually the convoy stops near us because they're heavy vehicles and find it difficult to get the right gear up some of the hills. We then walk out in front of the vehicles – usually a control vehicle or a missile launcher – and hold up our banner. The vehicles are very large and very menacing. I still shake with fear when I see them. We hold the banner in front of the vehicle because we feel we're saying to the driver: What you are driving can kill millions of people you will never see. Well, you can see us, are you prepared to do what you are trained to do? – to make them question why they are in cruise missile vehicles. We have nearly been run over once; usually the police dive at you and throw you out of the way, or twist you into armlocks so that you can't move unless you want to break your arms or your back. Or they hold you on the ground with your face in the dirt. Sometimes these attacks are very sexually orientated; they are always abusive to your body and your head. Often they get one person on their own in a police van and intimidate them.

We shake when we see the convoy coming. For most of us the sound of the quiet broken by the outriders' motorbikes purring fills us with fear. I'm still terrified by the police and the courts. I try not to be, and I certainly don't let them know it because, as my lover says, then they really are punishing us, and that's what they want: to make you too scared to protest.

Sometimes we hide in ditches (usually with nettles in) then mark the vehicles with paint or rotten eggs. We did this on Hiroshima Day (the convoy always comes or goes back on Hiroshima or Nagasaki Day). We've also been into Aldermaston (a nuclear research centre) and left leaflets and a summary of accidents related to Aldermaston for the workers to read because they're not told about them.

All the actions we do are non-violent, physical and verbal. When we decide on an action we have to plan it very carefully and check the possible consequences to us and others. And if something unexpected comes up we will stop the protest rather than put someone in danger (including the police and military). I've learnt a lot about non-violence and it's very important to me as a way of life and a vision of the future – not just living passively but being involved in non-violent direct action; seeing non-violence as a very positive way of changing the world. Using your self, changing your self and consciousness and then challenging the power behind a violent society. If we can each be responsible for our own violence, then maybe we could change the violence in the world.

Being able to respond non-violently to the police is very hard. It's funny, but it's easier to hit someone than to avoid having a violent response. To let yourself go limp within the police's hold, but still maintain your right to be in the place you want to, so you can do your protest but not engage in a power struggle with them, takes a lot of thought and inner conviction. If you're violent, there's no difference between you and them, except they've got a bigger weapon. You have to look at yourself and question motives, inner prejudices and years of conditioning. On my own I couldn't do these protests; I totally trust the woman I love and live with. I trust her to share the horror and fear that the convoy and the police bring into your life (often your sleep). Non-violence is about your everyday life as well. Both of our boys have been brought up without any guns or war toys. We didn't want them to learn that killing is just a game. We want them to know that they don't have to be aggressive just because the world expects boys to be.

One of the best parts of the eighties was the end of 1986 when the INF treaty to scrap cruise missiles was signed. What we had been working for had been achieved. On the night it was signed a friend had organised beacons of fire and hope to be lit all over the world as symbols of peace. We carried tyres (heavy ones) up a hill and set fire to them and stood round and hoped that change could continue. This was very special because my lover's mother and father came and our two children, so it was in a way three generations working for peace and celebrating the first time a backward step has ever been made in the nuclear age. In April 1987 the treaty was finally ratified by American Congress and the Soviet Assembly. We celebrated then too. The convoy is still coming out and we still stand by the side of the road – not so much now, because now that it's obsolete we don't feel the manhandling we receive is worth it. It will be a few years after the ratification of the treaty before cruise is finally broken down into its component parts and rendered useless, except for the nuclear warheads which will be reused in other nuclear weapons.

During the eighties I learned all the foundations of my political consciousness. What I learned is not what Thatcher wanted model people of her Prime Ministership to learn. Laws such as Clause 28 and the Public Order Act were all made to control the population she sees as subversive. I hope I continue to be subversive and work towards a world I'd enjoy living in, instead of the one I despair of when I read newspapers or watch the news.

8

Coming of Age

Agnes Quashie

What I now write surprises me, as much as it may surprise those who know me and those who are close to me. This is because, although I always write from 'myself', I have never actually writen about 'myself'. When I write I often ask myself, 'In what voice shall I speak?' This is principally in academic work where I find problems because I have internalised the need to observe at least some academic essayistic etiquette. Writing this piece makes a real change for me because it does not present the same problems, but this is not to say that it does not present any problems whatsoever.

Before I could consider what I wanted to include in this piece, I first had to decide whether I wanted to write it. This is because, if I am honest, I have become quite cynical about Blackwomen[1] producing a certain type of experiential writing that is too often marketed for a white target audience. Moreover, I had to come to terms with the problem that if the book was to be aimed at a wider audience that would include Blackwomen, should I really write something that was negative, since so much of what Blackwomen find available to read at the moment is of this kind. This is not to say that writings which concentrate on the negative aspects of our lives are invalid and should therefore be condemned; in fact I think such writings are very necessary as they illustrate to us just how resilient we are – such writings inspire us and give us strength. It is just that I feel that at times something positive has to be said also. This dilemma was resolved for me when I came to the conclusion that it is possible to turn negative experiences into positive strengths. The decision to write this piece also gave me the opportunity to capture some of the experiences I have had during my life whilst they are still going on, so that those things that I can salvage and learn from them are not forgotten before the learning process is already over.

I am well aware that in writing about my adolescent years, I will read an adult interpretation into them. However, writing is always a retrospective act and it is therefore impossible to avoid a 'retelling' of events. None the less, writing at this point in time allows me to reflect upon those years, and it permits me to come to terms with the social and political effects of 'coming of age' in Britain under a government which was epitomised for me in the name of 'Margaret Thatcher'. Indeed, this piece does not have any other overall unity except for the fact that my perception of the past ten years has been tarnished by this name.

Two things stand out in my mind as being of particular importance when I was growing up. The first was 'the Church' and the second was my education. During my childhood and for a part of my early adolescence going to church or being forced to go to church was a regular occurrence. It is difficult to remember a Sunday on which feigning illness actually worked. As regular as clockwork the 'Sunday School' van would turn up at 10.45 a.m., my sister and I would be taken to church, and we would be there on our best behaviour, looking neat and tidy in our white crocheted berets until it was all over at 2.30 p.m. At this point it was time for the

Sunday School van to take us home, in the company of our mother who had joined us after the classes. I remember that I really hated going, first because I was always hungry well before the service had finished; but the real reason was that I was always anxious that I might be seen entering or leaving the church building by one of my school friends. I remember that my conversations with my mum often revolved around why were we forced to go to church, and that if God really existed and was so judicious why did so many disasters happen around the world and why were there so many people without homes and food. In all honesty these questions were not designed to be political at the time, rather I thought that if I could catch my mum out it would be a way to avoid going to church. For a long time this did not work, as going to church was the one thing she was really strict about. My mother's stock responses to these questions were 'Have faith' and 'The Lord will provide'.

At the time I could never understand how anyone could purport to have that much faith in their religion, and although I was dubious then, as I am now, about institutionalised religion, my understanding of these events has changed. Of course people from different cultures worship in a diverse number of ways, but in relation to my upbringing and the memories I have, it was more that people felt a need to have faith in something, and a need to take sanctuary and identify with something. This was always very important. I still see people today, who attended the church, and who still attend the church, real stoics of my mother's generation, who do not necessarily sit back and accept those events that happen around them as a result of 'our' government, but rationalise these things as tests that 'our Maker' has created in order to try us. I have come to the conclusion that in a country in which you are alienated, you have to, in many ways, admire such stalwart attitudes, even if you do not agree with them. Being a member of a Pentecostal church congregation gives you a share of something in which you belong; it is a belonging which, as a displaced Black person, you will be hard pushed to find in any other kind of institutional set-up.

School days are reputed to be 'the best days of your life'. If I remember correctly, they are supposed to be the 'halcyon days' of your youth. But for most kids who have grown up over the last ten years this statement will probably seem redundant and such nostalgia just a luxury. How weighted these words have now become! Since 1979 the word 'redundant' is like a term of abuse and the word 'nostalgia' merely jars when it is uttered. For me and for so many people of my age it is probably a word that we know the literal meaning of, but can give little meaning to. My school was single-sex and housed about 1500 girls; you always had the feeling that things would be less cramped if there were several hundred fewer girls in the building. There were regularly between twenty-eight and thirty-two girls in each class, and the only reason you volunteered to be a book monitor was so that you could make sure you had a book to yourself, ideally one that was not ripped or scrawled upon.

The area that surrounded 'my' school was made up of one huge housing estate that seemed to go on for ever. It was the type of housing estate that was always appearing in Thatcher's characteristic 'Government Report On . . .', the type of report that the government frequently produces but the type that solved/s absolutely nothing. In fact I knew quite a lot of crude statistical information about the estate, and as each new piece of information 'got out' it was circulated during break times. When you heard such news you were supposed to feel pity for, or superior to, the girls who were unfortunate enough to live there. Therefore to hear that the estate supposedly had one of the highest number of 'tranquilliser users'; to hear that it had 'a drug problem'; to hear that you could not get credit if you lived on the estate; and to hear that minicabs and taxis would not take you into the area came as no surprise, but just what you came to expect of the place. It is this expectation, in retrospect, that sickens me the most.

It is some years since I left that school and things have deteriorated considerably. Both the school and the estate are still standing, and many of my school friends still live on the estate and in the surrounding areas. Many of them have children, who may well end up in the same school as their parents if the current climate does not change radically, and soon. It is at times like this that I feel 'guilty' about writing these things as if they only happened to me, because I am only too aware that these experiences comprise the reality of too many people living in the current political climate.

There were a number of voluntary organisations in the area where I lived. The one that stands out most in my mind is an organisation which, as one of its many roles, campaigned and raised funds for 'Summer Play Schemes' for children in the locality. Due to the success of the Play Schemes, the organisation soon extended itself to providing a 'Supplementary School' aimed at Afro-Caribbean and Asian children, where they could come to be tutored in those subjects in which they lacked confidence. Of equal importance, however, the role of the Supplementary School was to counteract Eurocentric state education, by providing a cultural input into the education of those who attended.

My initial involvement in both the Summer Play Scheme and the Supplementary School was very basic, but at the time it seemed very exciting. During those years my perception of things was very localised, and it was not until some time later that I realised that Black people in many different parts of the country had set up, and were still setting up, similar organisations. To be realistic, it is obvious that there is an immediate need for us as Black people to create these types of organisations for ourselves: not only to fill the huge gaps in our education, but to provide positive images and some motivation for ourselves. However, there is now a part of me that realises the double-sided effect of this, because as long as we continue to 'provide for ourselves' the state conveniently fails to recognise the lack in its own provision.

There are a number of political events that provide the backdrop to my adolescence, most of which are negative, but all of which have only acted to strengthen my anti-government resolve. These are events such as the so-called 'Sus Laws', the government's three Immigration Acts, and the government's scaremongering about the disease AIDS.

One of the first policy decisions the Conservative government made was to give the police a very hefty pay rise. Growing up as I did with a very healthy disrespect and dislike for the police, I scoffed at this without rationalising until later just what the repercussions of the measure were to be on both a general level and a personal level. Living within the British experience has always been problematic for people of colour, but these problems have truly been exacerbated under the present government.

The Suspicion Law (1979) – or 'The Sus Law', as it was more casually known at the time – was yet another occasion when an apparently 'objective' Act of Parliament preyed on the lives of many young Black people. The law was enacted supposedly in order to provide the police with the power to stop and search any member of the public whom they believed to be behaving suspiciously, and who might therefore be about to commit a criminal act: but as you might guess, the suspects were usually young Black males, owing to some of the racist images held by the police of both the criminal and the potentially criminal mind. Now an investigation of most other offences – such as sexual abuse, which I regard as a great deal more serious than petty crime – requires that abuse is proven in order for something concrete to be done; therefore I could never quite understand why such arbitrary powers had been given to the police to be used prior to, and in the absence of, an actual offence. However, since the 'riots'/uprisings that took place up and down the country after that time, the brutal police interventions that helped to provoke them, and the violence that consequently ensued – as well as the police's characteristic 'handling' of strikes and picket lines – it has become clear why their wages were so swiftly increased, and why Maggie wanted/s to keep them so much in her favour.

The period during which this law was in effect proved a very anxious time for many Black families. Parents who were fearful for their adolescent children often attempted to impose informal curfews on them, hoping that the less their children were on the streets, the less opportunity there was for them to 'get into any trouble' with the police. Coupled with this was the embarrassment many parents felt when they were confronted by two police officers at their front door, only to be told that their son[2] was being held at the local police station. I can remember conversations I have had with brothers, sisters and peers, whose only response to this problem was to resist any attempts to be intimidated. However, more often than not this form of resistance, although understood and appreciated by many parents, frequently brought family conflicts, because in the back of their minds they could not really believe that the police, the public symbol of impartial justice, would intentionally pick on young Black youths. For many parents the very idea strained credulity, their principal concern being that their son/daughter did not humiliate the family by appearing in court; the racist nature of British society was acting, once again, to oversensitise us to the public image of being Black.

In ten years of government the Tories have found it necessary to pass three different immigration/nationality laws: in 1981, 1983 and 1987. Each of these laws has been overt and racist in its bid to define and redefine those who can become British citizens. Moreover, these laws have become increasingly brutal in both their 'official' implementation (e.g. the denial of the right to appeal against deportation on compassionate grounds, and the denial of the absolute right to bring in dependants) and in their supposedly 'unofficial' implementation (the use of virginity tests). These laws now act to define more stringently the 'them and us' of society.

It was the British Nationality Act 1983 that created the December 1987 deadline, by which all those people who held 'non-British' passports were required to register as British citizens. Anyone failing to do so faced the risk of deportation at any time, because now the 'right of abode' in the United Kingdom was guaranteed only to those who were 'eligible' and had therefore registered as British citizens. The requirements of this law were unclear to many people and the facilities provided by government organisations, as opposed to voluntary organisations, were very poor. The result was that many people like myself were forced to watch their parents, family and friends anxiously filling out forms, in order to ensure that one day they would not wake up only to find that they were faced with deportation. The humiliation involved for many people was immeasurable, as the media gave coverage of huge crowds of people gathering outside their particular 'offices of registration'. Like my parents many of these people have lived and worked in this country for decades, but once again they were to find themselves being treated like dirt.

It comes as no real surprise to me that this redefinition of who is classified as British came at a time when the Falklands was high on the government agenda. As past and current political events illustrate, nationalism and redefinitions of those who belong and of those who are tenuously permitted to belong are more often than not closely related; it is at times like this that national identity is of paramount importance.

To grow up and 'come of age' in a climate in which the government's preoccupation is for 'a return to Victorian family values' is bad enough. But to come of age when there exists the 'scourge' of AIDS, the acronym that has now become the government's moral watchword, is absolutely terrifying. The government's attempts to – supposedly – educate us through advertisements, circulars and 'public information' films have succeeded in turning a medical condition which has social repercussions into a moralistic social problem. For many young people of my generation the decision to indulge in sex has been laden with so many other burdens. Therefore, to be an adolescent 'immoral' enough to indulge in premarital sex, same-sex relationships or any of the other social taboos has held with it the prospect of being labelled one of the 'guilty' and 'deserving' victims, if you were/are unfortunate enough to contract the disease. For teenagers to reach an age when sex is an important topic at school, and for the word promiscuous to be an insult that has become synonymous with the word AIDS, give just a small indication of just how successful the government's 'educational campaign' has been. In fact, it has only been since the mid to late eighties that the message that anyone can catch AIDS has been 'drummed home'. However, for the most part this had been due to the public backlash created by the government's original hetero-sexist and racist campaign. Since 1985 'public education' has continued but the moral crusade has not disappeared; it has only become a much more subtle ideological tool.

Bringing this piece of writing to a close is extremely difficult, because I do not believe that I can make any real concluding remarks as the Thatcher era is not, as yet, over. Moreover, in view of the eleven years she has been in office, many of the statements that immediately come to mind sound extremely sophistic and clichéd. For those who know me it is probably quite humorous to think of me as being lost for words, but this is not because I have lost hope or given up, but more because eleven years of Thatcherism have worn heavily upon me, as upon many others. However, contrary to the image that her name and long period in office conjure up, I do not consider her or her government to be an omni-historical presence. Indeed, sooner rather than later we will see the demise of the Thatcher government, and this will signal the reinstatement of the party that now stands as its most likely alternative, under simple majority voting. Such a time will obviously be one of great celebration for the victims of her regime, but as a Blackwoman living in a society that acts to disadvantage on the basis of race, sex, class and sexuality I am not naive enough to think that a mere change of government will totally alter the position of Black people in this society. I am fully aware that this may appear to be a cynical statement, but in the foreseeable future our fight for a 'fair deal' will always be in process and negotiation; it will not be handed to us on a plate.

In the opening paragraph of this piece I argued that it is important and possible to salvage something positive from negative experiences, and although I am loath to accredit these things to the Thatcher government, many of the people I know, respect and have forged friendships with have emerged as a result of my experiences over the last eleven years. The past decade has proved to be a difficult time for all those people who refuse to be moulded into a product of Maggie's competitive and individualist ideology. This has meant that there are people all over the country fighting against this and more. It is the opportunity that I have had to meet just a small number of these people, and my knowledge of the fact that there are many more, that have made Thatcher's time in government just about bearable. The discussions, the heated arguments, the learning, the camaraderie, the sisterhood and the understanding I now have are symptomatic of the past ten years. Don't get me wrong – the Thatcher government is not 'responsible' for this; these people have always been there; however, they have become more visible to me because of the changes that circumstances have forced me to make in my life.

Notes

1. I have chosen to use the word 'Blackwoman' because at the moment it is the only 'label' that in any way encapsulates my reality. I decided to adopt this label after an interview with Barbara Burford in 1988, during which she explained to me that for her, the word 'Black' and the word 'woman' were two halves of one identity, neither of which could/can be subsumed within the other. I realise that the use of this 'label' might be considered reactionary, but if this is the case I do not apologise. This is because I believe that in the current political climate the use of such a 'label' is necessary. The only thing I would add is that I do not regard this 'label' as prescriptive or fixed, and I can envisage situations in which I would define myself otherwise. Indeed, I think it is important always to provide the space to be able to do so.

2. I have intentionally used the word 'son' at this point, not in order to endorse the use of the male pejorative but because young Black males were the members of the Black community who usually suffered directly as a result of this unjust and racist law.

9

A Deafening Silence

Louise Donald

This year I am going home. That's not exactly true. I am very definitely not going 'home' as in 'Wishaw, a small town near Motherwell, between Glasgow and Edinburgh, in Scotland' home. That place wasn't home even though I was born there and lived there for the first seventeen years of my life. I shall return to Glasgow, where I feel 'at home', which is a completely different thing, I suppose. I haven't lived in Scotland for twelve years. It's strange to see that figure written down. I regard myself as Scottish, yet I have chosen to live down South throughout the last decade, the '80s. True, all my essential family still live in Scotland: my younger sister Pat in Glasgow, my older brother Simon in Edinburgh, and my mum and dad continue to live in Wishaw, as they have done all their lives. I live down here in London, acting the part of the refugee and harking back to Scotland, all things Scottish and particularly all things Glaswegian. 'Oh, the people! Oh, the City! Oh, the SNP! Oh, it's so Labour-controlled! Oh, to be back home!' The truth is plain for all to see, and occasionally someone asks the pointed question, 'Why are you hesitating?'

There is something I have to ask myself: 'Why did I leave?' There were reasons, and they had a great deal to do with the fact that I am a woman, even if I didn't fully recognise that at the time. More than that – I would have denied that my gender had anything whatsoever to do with anything whatsoever. I remember tentatively suggesting in 1978 that Mrs Thatcher was good news, because she was a woman, but for God's sake I was only seventeen, and that was the full extent of my political analysis.

I have to believe that Glasgow will not be the same as Wishaw, now in the 1990s, otherwise I have no choice but to remain in London. Wishaw is a small town in Strathclyde, opposite Ravenscraig, the steel works which occasionally make the news, as part of Mrs Thatcher's proposed shutdown of the steel industry. The glow of Ravenscraig's furnaces can be seen from Wishaw Golf Club, at the foot of the town. It was once a mining village around which Wimpey homes were built – a place people pass through on their way to somewhere else: Motherwell or Hamilton or Glasgow. There was little prosperity. We lived in one of the posher streets, Coltness Road, in my great-granny's house.

There was NOTHING to do in Wishaw. *Emmanuelle I* and *II* played at the pictures until I left, as far as I could tell. You adored the Bay City Rollers, or you were nobody. Everyone read *Jackie*, unless you were male, and every Saturday we hit the Venturers Disco, in the Community Hall. The last number was always a 'Moon Dance' (slow song) and if you hadn't got off with someone by that time, you exited pretty fast. At school, you NEVER put your hand up to answer a question in class, because that meant you were a swot and a snob. I was seen as both. The teachers' job was to force you to speak.

I just couldn't get a foothold in Wishaw – I had to separate myself, because I wasn't entitled to be part of it. The boys were nicknamed 'Shug' or 'Rusty' or 'Mongo'; they had names, identities. The girls were a 'lumber', or they were 'hackit' (someone to get off with/considered ugly, definitely NOT someone to get off with). Potential lumbers who became actual lumbers then became 'whoors' (whores). There was little or no in-between status, as far as I could tell. This system all had a certain irresistible logic to it. I, as a woman, couldn't challenge the status quo. The last thing you should do was stand out in any way. Over time I became overwhelmed by the feeling of being used: picked up, used, dropped, used up. Sexual contact was furtive and unpleasant, saying 'No' was a contravention of every unwritten rule. It was why you were there, and so what!

Until I met Elaine. Together we could stand out, we could be bad. We determined to use boys, harder and faster than they could use us. It couldn't work, of course, and it didn't. It isn't enough just to break the rules, you have to establish a new order, something I was extremely slow to learn. She and I became more and more isolated, until we were known as the 'punks' and the 'lezzies'. Neither was meant as a term of endearment. We relished rejection, cutting our hair with garden scissors to look like Patti Smith, coating our eyes with kohl and wearing camouflage jackets with boxers' boots. Mum and Dad were well behaved during this period: they just closed their eyes when we came into the room. We invented our own initiation ceremonies, known only to us, and carried them out in the fetid secrecy of Elaine's bedroom. They were meant as symbols of our disconnection from the surrounding social structure, marks of the 'outsiders', emblems of our 'splendid isolation'. They were, in fact, a form of self-mutilation. To this day I have scars on my upper arms and the backs of my hands, where Elaine and I tore our flesh with broken glass.

I was seventeen and, unlike most at Coltness High School, I had the chance to go to university. The plan was to move as far away as possible; down South, if that's what it took. Anywhere as long as it wasn't this grey, dull, soulless landscape. Sheena Easton, from Bellshill, just round the corner, had the same problem, I suspect. Only she found Esther Rantzen, quickly followed by an American accent.

I went to York. Why, oh why, did I choose York University? Failed Oxbridge candidates abounded, and they were strange and alien creatures indeed. I immediately resorted to stereotype, getting excessively drunk on the first night and collapsing in a warren of corridors, unable to make myself understood. I failed every social examination within days. 'And Louise, did you try for Oxbridge?' they mumbled politely. Blank expression: 'Where's that?'

I didn't look right, I didn't sound right. I couldn't find anyone from Wishaw. I was the stranger. I wasn't allowed to forget it either. Received Pronunciation voices quoted Shakespeare's sonnets and picked texts apart in plummy tones, with sweetly rounded vowels. My vocal contributions at seminars and tutorials cut through the vapours of mellifluous harmonies, sounding harsh and jagged, even to my own ears. I had never actually heard my voice before. Now it echoed.

During one particular seminar, I replied to a point made. There was a resounding minute-long silence. Then the lecturer asked: 'Where do you come from, Miss Donald? Are you Irish?' The content of my comment didn't matter. It went unheard. I went unheard. The accent spoke volumes for them. It meant 'rough', or 'uneducated', or 'intellectually unsophisticated', or 'aggressive'. Eventually my accent was deafening to me. Speaking became an almost 'out-of-body experience', as I struggled to separate my voice from what I recognised as myself. I spoke less and less.

This was not an entirely personal issue, although it certainly had personal implications. Wishaw had led me to believe that my sights, as befitting a woman, should remain at some ill-defined but lowly level. I imagined that university would liberate me. I was nervous, but confident. I was greeted with a different sort of diminishment, and my sense of self seriously faltered. Reading seminar papers induced a panic I had never before experienced. People turned and focused, and I felt myself disappear. I was invisible as an individual, and publicly too. It wasn't just MY voice, MY accent, that were being ignored, but an experience of a culture different to the one being celebrated around me. I felt shame in my collusion with those who did not and would not understand. My vowels became rounder, my intonation less 'charmingly lilting' and my accent less 'quaint'. At the end of my first year I returned to Wishaw with an affected lisp, such was my confusion. I did not have the strength to insist on my culture as something legitimate or important, and so it gradually became submerged. I learned nothing.

That's not absolutely true. I learned little academically. I managed to manoeuvre through the course as anonymously as possible, and emerged at the end with a degree: a peculiar fact in itself. But I was exposed for the first time in my life to the word 'feminist', and had the chance to meet a few of them. Describing those women as 'them' makes them sound as though they were completely unlike myself. I did feel we had nothing in common, that their histories somehow made it possible for them to be feminists, but that mine couldn't accommodate the theory or the practice. Feminism seemed a student preoccupation, and could never be adapted to life in Wishaw. I agreed with almost all they said. I was pro-abortion rights, I knew that women were regarded as inferior, I saw men dominating everything, and yet . . . I wouldn't call myself a feminist.

I was firmly ensconced in a pattern of setting myself apart, of rebellion, that was hard to break. I wasn't going to join any club that would have me as a member. I could beat men at their own game, and I didn't need other women, with their support groups and never-ending sympathy and understanding, to help me. I was tough. I could do it alone.

I painted my bedroom walls in bright red gloss and the blinds remained drawn for the duration of my course. I holed up there and appeared on campus only when someone offered me a lift. I sat quietly in this cocoon, safe from the outside, undisturbed and disturbing nothing. *Time* passed. That was practically all that happened.

At the end of the three years, all of the few friends I had made in York moved to London. I traipsed after them, clueless as to what my next step should be. They were going into publishing, and taking secretarial or journalist courses, or going on to drama school. I did the rounds, dossing on everybody's floor (they all seemed to have a home in London) for months. There was a particularly curious stage during the Falklands War, when I camped at No. 11 Downing Street for a week. Geoffrey Howe's son was a friend of mine at York University. At this point I was a punk, with spiky, viciously backcombed blonde hair and a tendency to sport a particular pair of very attractive blue trousers, which unfortunately I had singed at the crotch with an iron: a large triangular singe in the exact formation of public hair. The security police, who stood constantly on guard, never failed to inspect my person whenever I returned to No. 11. The Falklands War was hotting up, and Mr Haig, the US Secretary of State for Defence, was in negotiations with Margaret Thatcher. I sauntered down Downing Street in my short-sighted haphazard way, only to be met by a pack of reporters, awaiting news about war developments from No. 10. There was a most embarrassing scene when I had to knock at No. 10 and wait for an age to be allowed in, so that I could gain access to No. 11. The cameras stopped rolling after they spotted the trousers.

Finally I found somewhere to live in Brixton. This period of my life is hazy and unclear. I was at my lowest ebb; expectations were nil, commitment of any kind was unthinkable. I seemed determined to realise an ambition of passing through my life and leaving no trace. I despised the ambitions and material success of my friends, convinced that I would remain unique in my self-abnegation and in touch with the 'reality' of the world. There was no coherence to my position, although I would have described myself as a socialist. I waitressed for a number of years, rising late in the day and working late into the night. The restaurant was a disco/fast food nightclub which stayed open until 3 a.m. The waitresses all wore black, with short skirts: our uniform. There was no basic pay, we depended on service and tips. This only made financial sense on Friday or Saturday night. On weekdays we would make £10 for eight hours' work, cash in hand. There was a central unit of women who supported each other when nights were particularly bad, and a peripheral group who never settled in and left soon after starting. The cashier was a man called Allie, who remained quiet and serene in the midst of a nightclub's sweat and noise. Admittedly he was safe in a protective little booth, but when we needed solace he was there to listen and comfort. He told us tales of fasting and purging on mountain tops and of the people of Brazil demonstrating against rises in public transport fares by walking to work *en masse*. Some of the other women saw him as a kind of 'wise man', but I remained sceptical.

I was getting stick at work from our ex-SAS manager because of my hair, which was matted with hair spray and stood approximately a foot above my head by now. He considered it unfeminine and too aggressively punky. I saw it as a symbol of resistance. Practically, it certainly was a problem in the rain, when it would unstick and collapse irretrievably. I whinged to Allie about the fascist manager and his sexist comments. Allie had a different analysis: I was constrained and limited by my hair and should shave it off and move on. 'What utter crap!' I thought. 'What is the stupid old hippy talking about?'

But something rang true. My 'symbols of resistance', which encompassed everything from my hair and clothes to my twilight and subterranean existence, had effectively held me motionless for five whole years. The anger and fear I felt were expressed in my appearance and the occasional outburst of uncontrollable rage. That anger was justified and necessary, but I had separated myself from the world I wanted to act in and change. Instead of shouting aloud and making demands, I was sullen and incoherent. I edged myself into corners of employment where I would have least effect, bemoaned my sorry lot and retired to bed, satisfied that I was being ignored.

My next job was as a cleaner. I have to confess that this was no ordinary cleaning job. An acquaintance of mine had been working for the Olivier family, helping them to clean and prepare their new house in London. He had to leave the country and suggested that I replace him. I was introduced to their interior designer, who was to give me the once-over. I got the job. Thus began two years as cleaner for the Olivier family. I was cleaning the 'best' toilets, polishing the 'best' silver, and nobody talked to me as though I was the cleaner – we would chat over lunch together – but it was more invisibility. As a cleaner, when you're working and 'someone' walks into the room, you leave the room.

I don't know why it was that my friends in London and my employers were from a class of extreme privilege. It had something to do with going to York and meeting the people I did; time and place. It also had something to do with the fact that somewhere along the line I had bought into their world and its value system. I had attempted to make myself acceptable to them. I certainly couldn't bear to be rejected by them. To an extent I had embraced those evaluations I rejected most volubly. I felt inadequate because I believed I was less than them.

I was struggling to pay bills and rent, because cleaners' wages don't go far: £2.50 per hour. Well, after all, most cleaners are women, aren't they? What would they do with a living wage?

The Oliviers' housekeeper was a young Scottish woman, from the Islands. She initially seemed wary and suspicious of me, but we became friendly over time. After some months, she confessed that her mistrust of me was due to the reference I had been given by the interior designer: 'Her name's Louise. She's Glaswegian, and seems a bit rough and common.' Hold on a minute! I've refined my accent, for God's sake. I've been to university. Some of my friends are quite posh. It was as if I was branded. And after all, I was just the cleaner. It all added up for him: Glaswegian = thick, cleaner = thick – in other words, totally thick. I realised then that I couldn't 'buy' into this class of manners and money, even if I wanted to. I needed their approval less and less, and began to feel a stubborn sense of pride about who I was.

His attitude is not exceptional or remarkable in the South of England. It is an expression of a general sense of innate superiority, and our implied inferiority, with all that entails for those at the receiving end. The 'our' may apply to those of a particular class, race or gender. It is the notion that Scots, for example, are not capable of depth of thought or feeling or understanding concerning anything other than our own parochial, and by definition narrow, lives. Our dialect and language, in both common usage and in our art, is granted no worth outside its natural borders – not only that, we are seen as wilful and deliberately obscure if we insist on maintaining it outside those prescribed limits. Except, of course, in the last couple of years, when a few individuals have become quite the trendy thing.

Things were becoming extremely difficult at the Olivier household. Jeannie, the housekeeper, was leaving to set up in business, and they were looking for a replacement. They eventually found one. I knew from the beginning that it meant trouble for me. The new housekeeper had strong 'beliefs' about unemployment and was convinced the three and a half million were scroungers. She had her suspicions about me, and we had some unpleasant exchanges around the question of: 'Why didn't I have a proper job, with my education?' I was a classic example as far as she was concerned. I just didn't want to work, that was the problem, Never mind the fact that I was doing a job she considered far beneath her. I knew I had to get out.

Pat, my sister, was unemployed in Glasgow at this point, but her experience of living on benefit was different to my life on low wages in London. She was living in a flat with five other friends, who were on and off the dole. This meant everyone had access to exactly the same limited resources, and curiously money almost ceased to be an issue. They went to the same pubs and cafes, because that's what everyone could afford, paid equal shares of the bills and picked up part-time work where they could. They didn't feel exceptional or odd because they were on the broo. Everybody knew the problems involved and there was some mutual support in that.

For my dad, it was different again. He had been made redundant twice already in the '80s, having worked for thirty years. There was no support for him, only an increasing sense of isolation as time went on and the prospect of work retreated further. He was now living on thirty pounds a week.

Maggie Smith, who was a good friend of Joan Plowright (married to Laurence Olivier), often came to stay at their home when she was rehearsing a play in London. We sometimes chatted in the kitchen as I cleaned the kitchen sink or washed their floor. I liked her. Her mother was from Anniesland in Glasgow, and we enjoyed putting on 'funny' Scottish accents together. She recognised the humour, because it was a part of her own history. Finally, she invited me to become her personal assistant and dresser throughout the production of a new West End play. The situation with the new housekeeper had become intolerable so I accepted the job with relief. I didn't like the play, but I loved Maggie. Thus began a stretch in theatre life, once again working late at night and sleeping through the day. I still hadn't emerged from the twilight zone. The job seemed mainly to consist of quick changes behind the scenes and hours of crossword-solving with Maggie, which suited me fine.

In 1987 my dad was made redundant yet again, for the third time. He was beginning to take it personally. Unemployment was a massive problem in Scotland throughout the '80s. Today the Conservatives like to pretend that the Job Club has put paid to all that. Unemployment is apparently not an issue any more. For my own family it wasn't until 1988, when my sister finally entered college, and 1989, when my dad found another job, that we were off the statistics for real. In many parts of Scotland, the dole is as popular as ever. You wouldn't know it from where I sit in London.

It had to happen, I suppose. I was beginning to feel discontented with my self-imposed lot of low wages and even less job satisfaction. I wanted to affirm my existence for a change. I wanted to effect change somewhere in the world, if that was possible. I wanted to speak, but I wasn't quite sure what I wanted to say.

I applied for the post of School Administrator at the London Contemporary Dance School and got it – a surprise to me, given that I knew zilch about contemporary dance. I wasn't exactly biting my tongue to restrain myself from raising my voice about modern dance technique, but the job gave me the sense that I could function fully and with some confidence. I didn't need to apologise for taking up space any more.

A friend who also worked at the School had recently become involved with the Campaign Against Pornography. She was excited at the prospect of a group of women forming an active campaign which would challenge certain attitudes at the core of our society. The idea that all women were defined as potential 'prey', as illustrated by pornography, simply because of their gender, was about to be questioned – loudly. How could we hope for freedom, in any real sense, when we couldn't get beyond our bodies? How could we believe that anyone heard us in any sphere of our lives, when we were rendered silent about the fundamental lies being told about us? How could we aspire to equality for women of ethnic groups, when they were being represented in completely racist terms by the images and text in pornography?

Her excitement was contagious and I wanted to be part of it. Here was something I wanted to shout and scream about, and I didn't care who heard me.

I had never been actively involved in campaigning before and it was an opportunity to work with women I liked and respected. I got stuck in. Within months it felt as though I had never NOT been campaigning. A full-time and demanding job was supplemented by meetings with never-ending agendas, and leaflet-writing into the night. To be honest, I wasn't up to much with the campaign strategies and documents, or the CAP literature-writing. I saw my role as entertainer for those who were exhausted and doing the real work during our late-night sessions. I watched a lot of television and so I became CAP's media monitor. This felt reasonably safe.

Late one Friday night, I accidentally tuned into the 'James Whale Radio Show'. I couldn't believe my eyes or ears. This man loves to humiliate women. This is his joy and pleasure and forte. He is very good at it. The Media Monitor (note I have gone upper case) immediately rang the Director of CAP: 'I've been monitoring the media. We have to do something, anything, about James Whale. I think we should call "Right to Reply".' 'Okay, Louise. Do it!' What, me? The person who only recently had a severe panic attack at a school faculty meeting? Nobody said anything about Media Participation, only monitoring. Well, I'd monitored, hadn't I? Oh God!

I phoned 'Right to Reply'. Worse was to come – they were interested. I wrote the minute-long video-box monologue, thinking, 'This is okay. Like a passport photo-booth or something. Nothing too exposed.' I took time off work and went to Channel 4 studios, with the support of CAP's Director. They liked the piece, but really wanted to get the Executive Producer of the show into a studio discussion. With me. They wanted someone else to read the video-box, and in the meantime they tried to persuade the makers of 'The James Whale Radio Show' to appear. I prayed that they would fail. I think I looked unperturbed throughout this frantic session. They had no idea what they were dealing with – how could they? I looked normal on the outside. I felt satisfied that they would soon regret putting me through this agony. I would cry on television and then they would be sorry.

I phoned a friend who agreed to come in to read the video section. The researchers said they would call me the next afternoon to let me know if I was due to go on, but it looked unlikely. The programme makers were resisting. I was elated.

On Thursday afternoon *they* were elated. It was on! We would record the discussion the next afternoon. I went to the doctor and begged for beta-blockers, drugs which suppress the physical symptoms of anxiety. The wonderful woman gave them to me.

Why this long, detailed description of me going on television? It meant I was going to have to speak, out loud, in front of thousands of people. We're not just talking about a seminar paper here, or a ten-sentence-long report at a faculty meeting. The woman whose breath left her body when she was listened to was about to address the nation. (I do know that 'Right to Reply' has a limited audience, but this is how it felt.) The Campaign wouldn't stand for such nonsense. I had to find voice for the women who switched the television off in total incredulity and disgust. For the first time it was important to me that I find the strength to say something and remain in focus.

I didn't feel strong. That evening, myself and a representative from a child abuse study unit met for the first time to go through our material. I know we both wanted to scream with terror, but couldn't allow the fear the take grip, in case we completely unnerved each other.

The next day we met in a café, just before we were due to film. We both took the pills, and entered the studios.

They miked us up, did a voice test. The Executive Producer, our enemy, appeared on a monitor. I remember thinking, 'I can just leave. I won't die, just because I get up and leave.' The programme was 'as live'. I wasn't. I can't remember anything else.

I was joined in the 'hospitality' room by two women from CAP. I had the strongest sensation of love for both of them.

The next afternoon I watched 'Right to Reply'. The Executive Producer was dreadful. We were good! I had won something for other women – and for me.

I am not suggesting that this was some miracle cure. That was it! There you go, a voice. Work for CAP involved many more such sweaty incidents. I consumed a bottle of beta-blockers within a month. *Once* I did a radio interview chemically unaided. I now knew that it was not impossible. Someone – somewhere – had listened, and that counted.

I feel as though I have finally broken through the cocoon which held me warm, but muffled. I seem to be breathing air at last, the medium through which sound waves travel. And I want to go back to Scotland, my home. Not, I hope, for nostalgic reasons. And not without strong reservations. If Scots remain unrepresented and unheard, politically and socially in Britain, then women are equally invisible in Scottish culture (not for want of trying to be seen). We have our own bigotries to combat – and there seems to be a reluctance to expose those prejudices publicly, in case we justify the contempt in which we are held across England. The fact that Scotland has voted in landslide fashion in the last two elections for Labour, and sometimes for the SNP, does not make us a socialist state camping in enemy territory. We loathe the Conservatives, but we are conservative. Nowhere is this more obvious than in prevailing attitudes to women. I am hesitant about returning because, as yet, I have not established contact in Glasgow with those women who are in the process of naming and debating the issues. But I am optimistic! I don't intend to lose my voice again.

10

Learning a Different Language

Sharmila Mukerji

What I am writing here is a personal account of my experiences over the past ten years, while Margaret Thatcher has been in power. This covers my life from the age of eleven to the age of twenty-one, a particularly impressionable period and therefore, I feel, a valuable one in assessing Thatcher's influence on her children.

The influence of Thatcherism has been felt all over the country; fundamental changes have been enacted within this society, with far-reaching and sometimes devastating effects. But the most poignant influence has undoubtedly been that which has affected young people growing up in the Thatcher decade. It is us who will carry forward or initiate the ideology of the future: has the doctrine of Thatcherism set into our way of thinking, or have we been incited to overthrow this system? It is through us that the legacy of Thatcherism has the option to continue.

In writing this, I find that an autobiography is a difficult task, particularly when it spans only ten years in a relatively short lifetime and those ten years constitute my immediate past, with little opportunity for hindsight. The basic material I have does not submit itself as revolutionary or remarkable, yet I feel that it has some importance as a personal comment, a unique account of one person growing up in the Thatcher decade – possibly an insight into how the philosophy and policies of the Thatcher government play their own part in the upbringing of future citizens.

I was brought up in an untroubled, conservative village on the outskirts of Birmingham. My father, the only Asian person in the village, is a doctor at the district hospital; my mother, who is English, works at home. I went, at the age of eleven, to King Edward VI High School for Girls in Birmingham, which was to be my focal environment for the next seven years. After a successful audition for London Contemporary Dance School, I forsook my previous option of medicine and chose to study dance.

My father is Indian; that made me different. Racism can be vicious and confusing. For children especially it can create a hardness in their character as a defence against this attack on their existence. Cultural tolerance has in some ways improved since my father came to Britain thirty years ago, but racial prejudice has shown itself to have deep and spreading roots within our society. Laws recognising the rights of ethnic minorities have been passed, but this doesn't dispel the continuing tension which exists between the racial communities which constitute this country, exemplified by the riots in Liverpool and London. This seems to be a problem whose solution requires patience and effort as well as a recognition of its severity. Why do these riots break out? Has anything been resolved during the Thatcher decade? It seems that prejudice is still boiling beneath the surface layers of our society.

It appears that ethnic minorities in Britain have a choice: to follow, down to the smallest detail, every aspect of their native life that they can re-create here in Britain, and bring their children up in that tradition; or to abandon their culture in an attempt to integrate with this society.

My parents' concern about and experience of racism prompted them to shield their children as much as possible from this prejudice. This was one of the reasons they sent us all to King Edward VI schools, as an educational insurance against racial intolerance. Their experience, the hostility against their mixed marriage, was also to have its effect on us: as a safeguard our Indian origin was hidden to a great extent. My parents had felt the hostility of racial prejudice, and I grew up knowing very little about this alien Indian culture, which provoked so much ill feeling among some of my fellow countrymen and women.

I was dominated by Englishness; my feelings strove towards acceptance in this genre. My education and my upbringing were undoubtedly English, and the culture which I came to recognise as my own included none of my father's heritage. I grew up with incredible ignorance in this respect, not knowing my father's family or even where they were living; we never visited India. And so it turned out that the attempt to defend me from the aggressive racism my parents had experienced dissociated me from their background. This not only deprived me of a fascinating cultural wealth, but also left a separation in my relationship with my father and an insecurity within myself. It may seem bizarre that until recently I didn't feel the urge to discover this hidden background, stored away for so long, but I grew up not recognising that anything vital was missing until later on when my own imagination and ability to observe was kindled, and with a greater perspective I could identify the pieces which had been missing. But I am relieved that I have finally come to this realisation. I am excited and fascinated by the search that lies ahead, not only for the vastness of the culture, but also for my place in it. My aunts, uncles and cousins whom I have never met – they are indeed long lost. Their existence is so far away, yet we are linked by the same blood; we have a relationship without ever having met. It lies ahead for me to discover this relationship with India. Will I find connections, will it be possible to establish these links? Is there something in my genetic or emotional structure which will enable me to share a sense of identity with the people of this nation?

I entered King Edward VI High School at the age of eleven, and embarked upon this stage of my life with a strong sense of privilege and with the knowledge that out of it I was expected to emerge with success in the academic field. The school provided what was essentially an academic training; it produced some of the best results in the country. It was selective, we were privileged with our education, although I wonder how many of us actually realised what that meant. We never had any disruption of our study, facilities were first-class, equipment was never lacking, and the teachers were highly qualified and rarely involved in any kind of strike action. It was an extremely comfortable environment; there were very few external barriers between us and the expected success.

However, it was also a very protective environment. Most of the pupils came from upper-middle-class families. I never experienced the harshness of what was happening outside my school environment, since unemployment, strikes and demonstrations rarely directly touched me, my friends or our families. Throughout my time at school I became more and more frustrated with my own passivity, and by the emphasis placed on examination success. I became increasingly aware of my limited range of thought, centred very firmly on my life and activity within the school. We operated in relative isolation there, unaware and inexperienced about political consequences: unemployment, cuts in public spending (our education was safeguarded by private money), racial tension, which never really surfaced within the predominantly white school, and strikes, which I think few of our parents were involved in.

Being at an all-girls' school did have its advantages. What I took from there was a sense of my own capabilities, the reputation and achievement that attended such a traditional education. I could identify the possibilities that lay open to me through my qualifications, the opportunity to reach the top. We were expected to fulfil our potential as people going out into the world, not merely in the role designed by society for women. Therefore we could aim to be professional individuals. Ninety per cent were expected to go on to higher education; that was the norm, and in fact very little information was available about going straight into a job, or the more practical higher education courses. There was a pressure from the tradition of the school and its academic record for us to seek the most prestigious careers. It was treated almost as a foregone conclusion that we would continue along the conveyor belt from school to university to career.

While I was faced with the dilemma of choosing a career, it inevitably made me examine more attentively what I thought I would be happy doing for the rest of my life. Would it be one career which I would rigidly stick to in order to establish myself, or was it possible to juxtapose several interests? I chose medicine. I was doing three science A levels, and this option satisfied many of my concerns. The strongest of these was my desire to work in the Third World. I felt a responsibility to help on a personal level, since I realised that it was through the inaction of countries such as Britain that help had often been denied, or through their dominant intervention that livelihoods had been sacrificed for profit. I saw that this was an area which could be immensely fulfilling, not only serving as an opportunity to return some of the fortune that I had received with my circumstances and education, but also giving me the opportunity to learn about cultures which are difficult to comprehend from the relative ease of our own society. Medicine was also in the family; both my parents were involved, and on my father's side there was a strong medical tradition. This at least gave me some experience of what the medical profession would entail in terms of work demands.

The choice of medicine turned out to be a very popular one with many of my fellow students. I suppose that prestige and financial gain helped to influence some decisions, and it was definitely a respectable mainstream profession to choose as far as the school was concerned. However, even though we had every encouragement within the school as to our capabilities, I found that outside the school it became significant that we were women. Medicine is a tough profession, but even more so for women, who have to put up with dismissive attitudes concerning their role in family life. I was asked at one of my medical school interviews how I felt I would be able to combine a medical career and children. Were children really to exclude me from participating in professional work? Of course not; if I was going to have children the childcare would be equally shared – did they not see this as a viable option? Did they put the same questions to the male candidates?

Career choice is really a difficult problem. Most of us had so little experience outside school life that it was hard to know just how well matched we would be to the careers we were choosing from within the security of our home and school. Pressure from outside surely has an influence as well. The policies of the Thatcher government do not encourage education for its own sake, as an education for life; rather they are concerned with the profitability of the educated people: how they can contribute towards building up the wealth and efficiency of our country, which will then be concentrated in the hands of the few who have been most successful. Secure careers are therefore much more favourable options, since it is becoming increasingly difficult to survive in this country without personal wealth. Careers are a means of protecting the individual, providing you channel your efforts into the right field. We are under a threat that if we don't look after ourselves, no one else will be there to do it for us; unemployment during my experience as a young person has stood as a stark fact, and the numbers of homeless people reflect the lack of concern for those who can't cope in such a system. Emphasis is placed on the individual and on the importance of profit and efficiency.

At school I felt that I knew nothing, despite examination success. I wanted to find out more about myself, to challenge myself in an area with which I was not familiar. I wanted to know more about my environment and the society with which I felt I had little contact. I was lacking experience of living and felt that if I launched straight into medicine there would be scant opportunity to look in depth at the scope of my other interests. So I completed my medical application, for safety purposes, but my inclination led elsewhere.

My inclination was increasingly towards dance. I had always wanted to be a ballet dancer. Ballet had been scorned at my previous co-ed school, and I had had a hard time hiding my involvement, so at KEHS I decided to let everyone know right from the start that this was what I wanted to do. I don't think any of them took it very seriously; after all, we all had our own dreams – to be the first woman astronaut, to compete in the Olympics – so to become a ballet dancer was not that absurd. However, so far as I know, none of my school friends has become an astronaut or an Olympic medallist!

Nevertheless, my enthusiasm for dance continued and through the dance lessons at school, once a week, I became more interested in a freer style of movement. I had struggled with the extreme technique of classical ballet, since my physique was not naturally suited to it, and to find a new way of moving which emerged more naturally was exciting and stimulating. A dance workshop was started by a teacher at school, and through her imagination and guidance it proved to be very popular, although at first it was not treated as a serious extracurricular activity. This involvement gave me some of the most enjoyable opportunities for performance, and revealed contemporary dance as a fascinating medium to explore. Dance gave me the the opportunity to break away from the conventional academic expectations that the school had for us. I became absorbed by its variety and the enjoyment I got out of both preparing and performing. I saw dance as a way of broadening my horizons; it gave me a sense of direction, and a way of establishing my own identity. At the end of my final year at school, I auditioned successfully for London Contemporary Dance School. I had already been offered five out of six applications for medical school, and was successful in my A levels that summer, but the attraction of this alternative was potent.

Although some people thought I was throwing away all my opportunities and wasting my education, I found that the decision to choose dance against all odds was not as agonising as might have been expected. I know I was very fortunate to have been able to make such a choice without feeling that I was called upon to sacrifice one option in favour of the other. This liberty was endorsed by my parents, who did not try to persuade me either way. Although they knew little about the dance option, since they were both involved in the medical profession they knew its demanding nature, and the total commitment that was needed. My father's advice was to think carefully, make my choice, and then concentrate wholeheartedly on that decision so that I could achieve the best that I was capable of.

In comparison with other dancers I had enormous back-up. My parents paid for my living expenses in London; some dancers had to work during vacation and term time to support themselves or even take a loan. How would they ever manage to pay that off? I also had the security of good A levels and, having already been through the medical school procedure once, I relied on myself to be able to do it again if necessary. And I had the tolerance of my parents in letting me make my own decisions.

Had I not had this insurance behind me, would I have been prepared to sacrifice everything for dance? That would have been a tough decision, and one which I would have felt pressure from the economics of this country not to take, since dance is not a means of financial survival. But the experience I have gained through this training is surely worthy of some recognition: personal experience which emerges from a philosophy of not only training to be an artist, but training for life. It is this principle that the school is based on, and it makes immediate sense, since art is an expression of life. I feel that whatever I go on to do, I will have benefited enormously from this freedom to participate in a pursuit which exists outside the sphere of mere financial advance.

This experience doesn't seem to count very much in the present government's scheme; arts are not valued or materially rewarded unless they bring commercial gain. The influences which are shaping our world today are based on a concern for profit, for the status of Britain, on a global scale; concern that we keep up political appearances, that we defend ourselves against our neighbours, and against responsibility for our neighbours. There is concern for the outward appearance of the country, but this belies the jobless and homeless people within, and the physical destruction of the country itself.

One of the realisations of my generation must be not only the demise of culture, but also the starvation of all areas of non-profit-making activity which are none the less essential in our lives. The health service, other public services, and education have all been subjected to reform in order to try to make them more economical, even at the cost of those who rely on them. Conservation has now managed to force its way into politics through the immediacy of the environmental crisis on an international scale. Even so, token gestures on the part of the government and industry are the most they are prepared to give in order to safeguard their short-term profit.

I feel that the desire for profit is governing our country. Is this what we live for? For many of us, I think not. But those in power are making decisions otherwise, evaluating the activities of one person as more profitable than those of another. The arts in general are undervalued. Grants are awarded to establishments of high culture such as the Royal Ballet and the Royal Opera, but the funding of smaller companies is very short-term, often operating on a project-funded basis, discouraging the sort of experimentation which is needed to vivify an art form.

Janet Smith, a contemporary choreographer and dancer, pointed out to me the differences which she has found over the ten years during which she has been working. Initially, in 1976, she had difficulties in obtaining funding since contemporary dance was such a new phenomenon, unknown and therefore a financial risk. Nevertheless, she found that it was possible to find some way of surviving while she established herself and her company. In 1988 her company, Janet Smith and Dancers, was disbanded despite being highly popular, because of a withdrawal of minimal, but essential, funding. Dancers have never had an easy or secure career, but whereas previously it was possible somehow to survive alongside dance, now even basic survival, limited to accommodation and food, cannot be guaranteed. Dancers, judging by some opinions, are expected to work out of a sense of duty or devotion, without any financial support or respect for their creativity or contribution to society. The commitment required by dancers is enormous; they have to be prepared to give everything for their art, with little outside appreciation. There is also a time limit imposed on all their performing career, and there is very little you can show for the hours dedicated to this performance art after your career is over.

It makes an interesting comparison to look at the attitude to dance further afield. In many countries dance is not alienated from society, it is an integral part, no matter what the economic status of the country. In Indonesia dance pervades everyday life through the use of it as a reflection of religious beliefs and accepted social behaviour, demonstrated in the form of a community activity. Dance forms an important part of daily worship in the temples; everyone knows what the dance is about, and recognises its significance. Not only in non-Western countries is this respect shown. In Germany every town has its opera house; dance has grown up in this environment and therefore has a natural role within the community. Dance is an established and respected profession: dancers have enough money to live on and they are able to survive by their work.

Contemporary dance permits an unlimited opportunity for expression through movement. Not only does it encompass movement, it has the freedom to combine movement with any other art form; music being the most obvious, but film, speech, sculpture and video have also been used. (This combination of arts was in fact initiated by the pioneers of contemporary dance at the beginning of the century; Martha Graham worked in close conjunction with Nagochi; Merce Cunningham with the composer John Cage.) However, this freedom can be intoxicating; you have to search hard to preserve the integrity of the movement, since its strength lies not in the individual components of the work but the way they are put together. It may be tempting to hide behind iconoclasm, but originality should not be the dominant criterion by which such work is assessed since this can lead to self-indulgence on the part of the choreographer. If the dance becomes entirely self-referential, the movement can be appreciated only by practitioners of dance as a technical presentation, which seems to lose its purpose as a performing art.

The power of movement in expression is undeniable – take, for example, the captivation of young children by ballet. The fact that children can be attracted by such a formal style as ballet surely gives an indication of the instinct they have for movement, and therefore the potential that movement has for expression and communication. At an early age, children seem extremely receptive to movement; what is it that causes us to have such inhibitions about it later on? It may be because of the preference given to more direct forms of communication, and also the restriction of our movement as we become more self-conscious (lose the freedom of childhood). Dance has yet to be fully recognised, not only as an art form but also in education. In school, children can be given the opportunity to participate in dance in an informal situation. This is one valuable way of growing up with a more conscious awareness of our bodies, and dispelling some of the inhibitions which may creep up on us if we lose this connection with expressive movement; this should break down some of the barriers of elitism which can surround dance.

Dance is a transient art. It cannot be captured or frozen; it is for the moment. This is one of its greatest attractions. It demands from the audience the recognition of expression through movement, and relies on creating an instinctive and immediate response within us. However, the ephemeral nature of dance makes it difficult for it to become recognised or appreciated at a later period, since recording on film or video inevitably loses the distinctive qualities and vital experience of the live performance itself.

Dance has opened up much of myself for examination; the discipline of intensive physical training gives you not only physical stamina and agility but also a mental stamina and a driving force behind your actions, a closer understanding of the effort needed to produce the best, and an acceptance of nothing less. The nature of dance makes it difficult to assess progress and define achievement, in comparison to similar physical training in sport, where there are definite goals to aim for: records to beat and medals to win. But the absence of such measures of success makes dance particularly valuable, since this encourages a constant re-examination of the art and of the individual. It develops individuality rather than self-indulgence, since it necessitates establishing a relationship between performer/choreographer and audience, and therefore has the potential for communication and change not only for the individual but also within the society.

Through my training I have come to realise many things about how I function, how I react under pressure; I have developed a respect for myself, and a better understanding of my own weaknesses. In these respects, my training in dance will prove of lifelong value in whatever fields I wish to participate. In my first years at the school I was confronted with the enormous switch from mental training to an essentially physical approach; thoughts and mental processes have to be translated into movement, which necessitates a very different procedure from that to which I was accustomed. As a dancer, not only do you need to have the artistry to create and perform movement but you also have to make your own instrument, train your body, and push it to its limits; there is nothing else, no paint or musical instrument ready-made that you can rely on. It takes effort and dedication to put yourself through five hours a day of physical and mental strain; no wonder that you at least find out something about yourself. It took me quite a while – longer than I expected – to adjust to this new education and to realise how much potential the body has for expression, and how this can be translated into movement.

One of the attractions of dance is its potential for communication. Communication through movement, through the use of our bodies, is inherent within us. Yet because of the emphasis placed on more direct methods of communication, in particular language (written or spoken), we underestimate our instinct for movement and fail to recognise its potential usage in our concentration on the more obvious (words). Contemporary dance, for me, aims to re-establish the significance of movement in communication, to use movement as a poignant and fresh comment on any aspect of life. From its very beginning, contemporary dance has commented on social issues and given a new perspective on them. Martha Graham, one of the pioneers, drew her subject matter from American life around the time of the big Depression (in the late 1920s and the 1930s) and also focused on the experience and myths surrounding women – for example, in her portrayal of subjects as varied at St Joan and Clytemnestra, Emily Dickinson and Mary Queen of Scots.

I feel that dance is enriched by experience, from both the art world and our everyday lives. However, cultural and political ideas cannot simply be used as content for choreography; their significance lies in their interpretation through movement, and in a manner which is not argumentative or polemical, but rather more subtle in its exploration of the subject matter. For it is not the strength of the subject matter which brings power to a piece, but the way in which movement is found to interpret it. It was in this way that Martha Graham was so successful, since in her aggressive and angular movements she created a powerful expression of emotional suffering, tragedy and remorse which emerged in many of the subjects of her choreography. The movement itself is what we relate to emotionally; therefore it is this combination and creation of movement, rather than just the content of the piece, which makes dance available and relevant to the public.

Dance does not always need to comment directly on social issues but rather should seek to stimulate thought along new and varied channels. As Jane Dudley, a performer and choreographer who has participated in the growth of contemporary dance over the past fifty years, has said: 'Contemporary dance is based on the belief that movement language should be capable of representing the contemporary world, its attitudes and experiences, just as all art forms continually modify their modes of expression in response to the historical moment in which the artist is living.' This summarises the idea of integration that should exist between a dancer/choreographer and their society.

The portrayal of women in dance has been particularly

degrading. They were first seen as on the lowest rung of the ladder of virtue: as harlots, loose-living and promiscuous. Women in themselves were considered dangerous creatures; therefore to see them indulging in dance was the depth of immorality. Today the commercialism of dance exploits women as objects, presenting their bodies to relate only to sex, and as objects on display. Even during the nineteenth century this image was being developed to gratify the confused morals of the male audience viewing women on stage. Marie Taglioni, a revered artiste of nineteenth-century Romantic ballet, was considered by the rich male patrons of the theatre to be little more than a sex object; a nineteenth-century pin-up.

I have commented on some of the attitudes towards women in medicine, but are things any better in the liberal atmosphere of contemporary dance? From my position within that world I have the impression that attitudes are more advanced. The majority of dancers (and many choreographers) are women; and this art form was pioneered predominantly by women such as Isadora Duncan, Martha Graham and Doris Humphrey. There is a distinct lack of difference in training in contemporary dance between men and women; techniques such as the Graham technique require strong, powerful movement, and there is no distinction between steps suited to men rather than women or vice versa. Choreography is not bound by gender-stereotyped roles, as in ballet, but allows men and women to share equal roles not only in the type of movements, but also in supporting and lifting.

However, contemporary dance is still relatively unknown as an art form, and for many people dance is most popularly seen as ballet, the only dance form which has acquired the status of high culture. Nevertheless, from this position of art, ballet is restricted by the demands and expectations of the public, who expect and want to see reproductions of classical ballets such as *Swan Lake*, so that it has little opportunity for challenging those stereotypes which form a significant part of its tradition. Outside ballet, all other dance forms tend to be lumped together, steeped in a Middle Ages perception of dance as a low and base profession. Dancers are treated as worthless and exploited as entertainers for little reward. Public perception of women in the dance profession is low: they are engaged to display their bodies; this is perpetuated by the choreography and costuming of many of the West End shows.

Dance involves the creation of images, but I believe it also has the power to undermine images which persist within society. The centrality of the body in dance gives it the power to challenge views which are already limited and prejudiced. In challenging the representation of women, dance focuses on the body itself, which makes it particularly poignant since this is one of the areas in which women are most abused and exploited. Contemporary dance also has the opportunity to challenge gender stereotypes, since it is not bound by any tradition concerning the roles of men and women in dance, and can therefore undermine such stereotypes through choreography. Nevertheless, recognition of the expressive ability of the body is still limited, one of the problems that contemporary dance has to overcome through greater access and dance education.

As I come to the end of my dance training, I have a greater insight into the potential of dance. Dance is a powerful communicative medium, and I feel that its role in teaching and stimulating the imagination should be recognised. It has t ability to provoke thought, challenge opinions and inspire, particularly because of its use of the body as the instrument of expression, giving it a direct link with the audience. The elitism surrounding contemporary dance as a new art form needs to be broken down; people should be given the opportunity to participate in it through practical dance, and in so doing they should gain a wider understanding of the potential of movement.

Teaching dance to children can be one important way in

which this is achieved. My interest in this area has led me to explore community dance work – an attempt to break down the institutionalisation of the arts. Art should not be rarefied and treated as a separate entity, but should be able to exist with a purpose in contemporary society. We need to be aware of and involved in what is happening outside the dance world as much as in it, so that we have something to say as artists. There is a danger that because of its training requirements dance can become a studio art, removed from the outside world and therefore devoid of any communication links. I wish to avoid this isolation of dance from social and political affairs, since I feel that this has led to the essential individualism of dance becoming merely self-referential, thereby creating an elite, and in so doing starving itself of both audience and inspiration.

Under this government, individualism has been endorsed in the form of egocentrism which thrives on profit and the survival of one set of individuals over another. The perspective during the past ten years has been that of reshaping our society, changing its priorities to suit the economics of Thatcherism. The orientation during my time of political awareness under the Thatcher government has been towards valuing the individual over the community. Materialism is the dominating influence, especially in the form of privatisation, investing to safeguard our individual futures as much as possible, while those who cannot or do not operate within this mode have their support gradually eroded away from under them. I feel a strong link between the egocentricity that is apparent and the pressure which I felt bearing on us in our career choice – to lay aside our imagination and dreams, and concentrate on our individual survival. In this way the policies of the Thatcher government are felt most significantly in the influence they have had on the decisions and lifestyles of my generation. It is difficult to follow your own inclinations if they conflict with the long-term policies of this government. I managed only with the financial support of my parents, otherwise I might never have risked taking this opportunity to find out so much about myself and my potential in dance. But how many people could afford to take that risk alone?

My version of individualism seeks to recognise the value of experience, the benefit to society of allowing people to develop their individual talents – whether they will prove economically profitable or not – and giving them some way of feeding their knowledge back into the community while still being able to survive.

11

Disabled but not Dim

Alison Bark

I was born on 1 August 1965 in Warrington, Cheshire, England. When I was born I was very frail, as I was two months premature. Weighing 2lb 10oz, I was placed in an incubator. Without this I would probably not have survived, but something went wrong and while in the incubator I was given too much or too little oxygen – something which I am assured could not happen to a premature baby in England today. As a result of receiving the wrong amount of oxygen I suffered brain damage which, while not affecting my intellect, left me physically disabled.

For a long time nobody knew that I was brain-damaged and disabled, so this was not the reason why my natural mother – whose name I will not give here – gave me up for adoption. She already had two other daughters and her domestic circumstances were very difficult.

When I was four and a half months old, I was adopted by John and Patricia Bark, whom I will refer to as my parents from now on in this account. They already had one child: a son, Andrew Michael, born 20 November 1963, who was also adopted. He is not disabled in any way.

My new parents were delighted with me, because I was

quite pretty and talked early and fluently, but I did not learn to walk. However, the family GP said that as I was two months premature it was possible that my development would be two months behind that of full-term children. This pacified my parents' anxiety for a time, but eventually, when I was aged two years and two months, they became convinced that there was something seriously wrong. I could crawl, and I could stand if I was holding on to my mother's hand or a piece of furniture, but I could not walk at all. The GP sent me to an orthopaedic surgeon who diagnosed brain damage – cerebral palsy – spasticity. My hands were affected somewhat, but it had mainly affected my legs.

This was a shock to my parents, but they made the best of it.

When I was four years old I had an operation which enabled me, three months later, to walk for the first time. I was able to walk unaided once I had learnt, although my walk was not – and is not – completely normal, and I could not walk the same distances as other children.

Before the operation the education authorities had wanted me to be sent to a boarding school for disabled children, but my parents had refused. After the operation it was arranged for me to receive lessons for one hour daily from a qualified teacher who lived in the same road as us, and who taught me to read and write. Aged five and a half I began to attend the local primary school, eventually attending morning and afternoon for the same number of hours as the other children.

In my tenth year it became necessary for me to have another operation on my legs if the beneficial effects of the first operation were not to be undone.

After that operation I was still of primary-school age, but my parents decided that I should cease to attend the 'normal' primary school, and instead should become a pupil at a school for the physically handicapped which had recently been opened on the outskirts of Barnsley, South Yorkshire, a few miles from my home. All the pupils were day pupils, aged from three to sixteen. I attended this school, Rockley Mount School, until I was sixteen. I would have found it very difficult to manage at the local secondary school, which was much busier and larger than any of the primary schools in the area.

It is now completely unfashionable – at least in Britain – for physically handicapped children to go to special schools, even day schools. This was not the case when I was a child and teenager, however. I think I can see both disadvantages and advantages in this form of education.

It is said nowadays that a disabled child feels more 'normal' in an ordinary school, but as the only disabled child in the two primary schools I attended before Rockley Mount, there were times when I felt a bit of a freak, and a bit left out of things. At Rockley Mount all the pupils were disabled and most were more disabled than me, so for most of the time I felt more 'normal', not less.

As the whole school was geared to the needs of the disabled there was nothing in which I could not take part, from school trips to plays and carol services. In fact, in one school play I was the 'leading lady'. Although my speech and memory were normal, this would probably not have happened if I had been at a 'normal' school, where I would probably have been lucky to have been given a non-speaking part in the chorus. But at Rockley Mount even those confined to wheelchairs were given important roles in school plays, and children who could not speak at all were encouraged to become involved – taking the money at the door, helping to make costumes and scenery. All the school trips were to destinations which children who could not walk would enjoy.

Because there were far fewer children at this school than at 'normal' schools (approximately 125) much more individual attention was given to each pupil than would have been possible otherwise. Also, pupils were placed in groups for maths and English according to their ability, not according to their age. This suited me. My maths was poor, so I was placed in a group with children about two years younger than me, while because my English was above average I was placed with children two or three years my senior for this.

One of the disadvantages of the school, which may have been remedied now, was that academic teaching was poor, particularly in the sense that subject choice was narrow. There was no French or German, or any foreign language. The history teacher was not a specialist, her main subject being art. The home economics teacher doubled up to teach biology. There was not much physics, certainly nothing of normal standard. There was no chemistry, no economics. Religion was not taught at O level. In fact when, aged sixteen, I obtained an O level in English language, I was the first pupil ever to obtain an O level at that school. This seems incredible, when the school had been operating for several years, but it is true.

Instead of stressing the importance of academic achievement, the school placed a great deal of emphasis on sports. This is ironic, given that most of the pupils were in wheelchairs, and it may have been a form of overcompensation, for sport was certainly emphasised more than at most 'normal' schools. Many pupils, most of whom were not considered very capable academically, got most of their status and self-confidence from it, and it gave them a great deal of pleasure. I was not very interested in sport – I much preferred reading or writing stories. Despite this, I enjoyed swimming and was able to do this quite often as the school had its own swimming pool. I represented my own 'house', Wortley, every year in the school sports, and when I swam I sometimes won, but most of the other sports I participated in I did not really shine at.

When competing for Rockley Mount School against other disabled children's schools, I would throw the medicine ball, and/or take part in a 'walking race', and sometimes managed a second or third prize. In sports, however, I was paradoxically outshone by children more disabled than myself. Naturally, children confined to wheelchairs were far superior to me at wheelchair basketball, and other wheelchair sports.

In 1980 a few months before my fifteenth birthday, I went into hospital again, and had what is almost certainly the final operation on my legs.

In 1981 I took my CSE and O level exams. As well as passing my English O level I got through my CSEs, but I did not get a grade I in any subject except English, so I was not very well qualified. Nevertheless the Careers Officer recommended further education, so it was arranged that I should attend the sixth form of the secondary school near my home and try to get some more O levels.

The sixth form at Penistone Grammar School – which used to be a selective grammar school, but by this time was a comprehensive school – was housed in a separate building from the rest of the school. It was called 'Netherfields' and had once been an old people's home. Unlike Rockley Mount School, it was on two levels, but luckily I was capable of climbing stairs. As at primary school I was the only disabled student (apart from a girl with dyslexia). However, the disabilities of the dyslexic were radically different from my disabilities, so the school, in trying to cope with my needs, was really 'starting from scratch'.

I was a pupil in this sixth form department from 1981 to 1984. During my first year there I was doing their CEE (Certificate of Extended Education) course, and at the end of the year I obtained O levels in humanities, history and industrial studies. I now had four O levels, enough to enable me to do A levels, and so I went on to study English literature, religious studies and general studies.

I never expected to pass the general studies, which included subjects such as maths, technical drawing and physics – which I was hopeless at – but I did expect to pass religious studies, because I enjoyed the subject and was good at it. However, my exam technique was poor at this stage in my life, and I failed both. I was allowed to have extra time in examinations but what I really needed, I see now, was a break in the middle as my hands and body got stiff. I passed English literature, so I now had four O levels and one A level – not enough to enable me to attend an orthodox university.

I might have stayed on in the sixth form for another year and retaken the two A levels I failed – like my friend Susan, who also failed religious studies and needed this pass in order to get into music college. However, my father had obtained a degree with the Open University, so my family and I thought of this.

At this time the general rule was that a person under twenty-one could not study with the Open University, but this rule, which has since been changed, was waived in my case once my circumstances were known. It would have been silly if my studies had had to stop for two years at this stage in my life. It was agreed that I could enrol with the Open University from February 1985, aged nineteen.

Between leaving the sixth form and beginning my Open University studies I had some time on my hands, so I started a further education class in assertiveness training. All the people in this class were women, although the teacher had taught some mixed groups.

I suppose, as a young disabled woman, I subconsciously assumed that able-bodied women, especially older able-bodied women, were much more confident than me, and much more in control of their own lives. I was very surprised to find that these women – all able-bodied and in their thirties, forties and fifties – were so inhibited and repressed. They would not have their hair styled in the way they wanted, buy the clothes they wanted, take or change jobs, in case other people, usually the men in their lives, disapproved. We did not get around to discussing sexual problems – we concentrated mainly on problems like those above, and the best way to complain about bad service in shops. However, we were able to buy a book on assertiveness training in which sexual problems were discussed, and I was amazed and horrified to discover that many married and unmarried women had sex with men when they didn't really want it, because they feared that a refusal would make the men angry!

I was a bit of a feminist before I went to this class, but it confirmed and intensified my feminism. As a disabled person patronised by some ignorant able-bodied people, I see the stupidity of making assumptions about people merely because of their bodies, whether it takes the form of sexism, racism, ageism, or prejudice against the disabled.

I am very impressed by the way the Open University treats its disabled students. In the sixth form the staff had not been unkind or deliberately unhelpful, but they had not known what to do. The Open University, although most of its students are able-bodied, has had plenty of disabled students, provides a great many services which they can use, and is able to advise them.

It is compulsory to attend Summer School – a week at an ordinary university while the regular students are away for the summer. Generally speaking, if you do not attend you fail your course, but disabled students and others (e.g. those caring for disabled relatives at home) have a fair chance of being excused. However, the University prefers disabled students to attend unless it is absolutely impossible and so it allows them to take a Helper with them to assist them with dressing, eating, writing, or whatever they find physically difficult. The student either takes his/her relative or friend, or the University will try to provide a Helper from a pool of volunteers. Each time I have been to Summer School I have taken my mother with me as my Helper. The Helper's transport costs are paid by the Open University, and so are the costs of basic meals. A room is provided for the Helper if possible next to the disabled student, and they are usually given ground-floor rooms. There are also all sorts of physical aids, including – but not only – wheelchairs, which disabled students can ask to use during the week. However, last time I was at Summer School I met a man who had been silly enough not to tell the University that he was disabled, so he did not have a Helper or a ground-floor room, and found the week very difficult.

I have now done four Open University courses – by the time this book is published I expect to have done five. The Open University courses, if part of degree studies, last from February to October. They do not all require Summer School attendance. There are regular tutorials in the evening or on Saturdays – every week for new students – but most of the work is done at home. Nobody is standing over you, so you have freedom, but you also need self-discipline. I am now more than halfway towards my degree. For my exams I have not only had extra time but also a break in the middle for exercise, a snack and the lavatory. I have also been allowed to take my exams in my own home, with an invigilator sent out to me. Able-bodied students do not have these privileges. My studies have all been in the arts and social sciences, although maths and science courses are also available. (My father's Open University degree was mainly in geology.)

I have not learnt to drive yet, so have been dependent on being chauffeured about by my parents and occasionally my brother. My brother married in October 1989 and now lives away from home.

My social life has been rather restricted, to some extent because the disabled children I was at school with did not live near me, some living fifteen miles from my home. When I was sixteen I was invited to help with a local Brownie pack and after two years I gained my Young Leader's Certificate. I enjoyed this very much, but eventually after a change of leadership the weekly meetings became more craft-orientated and because of my limited co-ordination I wasn't able to contribute as much as before. Eventually I began to feel completely superfluous, so reluctantly I left.

After I left school I discovered the Barnsley PHAB Club (Physically Handicapped and Able-Bodied Club), a social club where I met again some of the children I had known at Rockley Mount School. This club did some quite enjoyable things, but most of the time it was boring.

I started to work out regularly at a health and fitness club in Barnsley owned and run by the former British athlete Joselyn Hoyt-Smith, who gave me lots of individual attention and was very nice to me.

In January 1989, following the deaths of both my mother's parents, we bought their house and moved to a suburb of Manchester. Having lived in a small town on the edge of the moors in South Yorkshire for twenty-three years, I found this a big change. However, I have not regretted the move. As we live near Manchester now, I am able to visit bookshops more frequently. Nevertheless it is unfortunate that they do not have more chairs or stools. It is difficult to choose between two books on the same subject when I cannot sit down to examine them, and my legs are starting to ache.

I have started to attend a local PHAB club, which I find more enjoyable and better organised than the Barnsley one. I am working on the Adult Leadership Scheme with a local Brownie pack. I am attending the nearest Anglican church – the church where my mother and father were married. (I was confirmed in 1984, having regained my faith after several years of agnosticism.)

Although I am becoming more High Church in my religious opinions, I differ from many Anglo-Catholics and Roman Catholics in wholeheartedly supporting the ordination of women. The argument that Jesus and his twelve apostles were male and therefore all priests should be is, I think, rubbish. Jesus and the Twelve were not Gentiles, yet most Christian priests are not Jewish-born and come from every race where Christianity is present.

The Roman Catholic hierarchy is more against women's ordination than the Anglican, yet this church makes the Blessed Virgin Mary a much more important figure than churches, such as the Methodist Church, which already have

women ministers. It seems that Our Lady is the Roman
Catholic Church's 'token woman'. They seem to think, subconsciously perhaps, that as long as she is prominent, it
doesn't matter if all other Catholic women are in a subordi-
nate position – while the 'low churches' seem to be using
women's ordination to prove that, while minimising the
Marian element, they are feminist. I can't understand why the
Catholic Church regards women as unsuitable to be priests
when according to the dogma of the Immaculate Conception,
Mary was the only created human being who never sinned.
(The sins of Peter – the first Pope – are clearly recorded in the
Gospels!)

I admire St Joseph because, according to High Church
belief, he respected his wife's decision to remain a virgin and
never forced her to have sex with him. Neither did he sexually
abuse the child Jesus, or commit adultery with other women.
I think his example is one that all husbands and fathers
should imitate, whether or not *their* marriages are consum-
mated, instead of whining that their sexual needs must always
be satisfied.

You will see from this that I think the Christian religion
can be interpreted in a feminist way, without traditional
beliefs necessarily being sacrificed.

Unlike some Christians, I am not against AID (Artificial
Insemination by Donor) for unmarried women. The Virgin
Mary herself conceived in an unorthodox way. Some people
assume that if you are considering the possibility of AID you
are either a lesbian or you hate all men. This is not always
the case. Some women would have been happy to have a
child in the conventional way, within marriage, but the
opportunity did not arise. Nowadays, with contraception,
abortion and sterilisation more readily available, it is easier
for women to have sex without later giving birth to a child.
Most people do not think that contraception is wrong, so if
you can have sex without having a child, why do they think
women should not be able to have a child without first having

sex? It seems cruel for women who are able to conceive children in the normal way to attempt to deny pregnancy and motherhood to less fortunate women.

I have not had many 'adult experiences', although I have voted and drunk alcohol. I have some difficulty regarding myself as an adult woman, especially as I look fifteen or sixteen – younger than my true age – unless I make a real effort to make myself look older. However, I have always known that I am intelligent, and so I resent the way some strangers assume that just because I am physically handicapped I am also mentally handicapped. I hope that this impression is dispelled as soon as I get into conversation, but I am rather shy, so I resent being forced into a more extrovert role than I would otherwise adopt in order to disprove these assumptions.

Looking back over the 1980s, I feel that I have made a lot of progress academically, but not very much socially and even less sexually. I hope this imbalance will be remedied in the 1990s. I am not naive but I feel that most of my knowledge of the world has come from books, newspapers and magazine articles rather than my own, very limited, experience. I hope eventually to learn to drive, which would make me much more mobile. I would like a satisfying career, which is why I am studying for a degree. I am determined to have a child one day, and I don't rule out marriage, although I am afraid of it. If AID for single women is made illegal, I may one day be able to adopt, as a single person, a disabled child whom nobody else wants, and who could benefit from my experiences. I may adopt a disabled child even if I marry.

12

Getting Here

Ruth McManus

This is supposed to be about 'growing up in the 1980s'. The story I tell has the backdrop of eleven years of Thatcherism, and is about my formative experiences and the changing conflicts of identity that have shaped my life.

I start in 1979, when I was fourteen and Margaret Thatcher came to power. I entered adolescence with three deeply embedded expectations about life. These were that life didn't involve difficult decisions, that it involved work but that if you worked hard you would get on, and that life was to do with 'falling in love' – everlasting, of course – and living happily ever after. I did know that adolescence wasn't supposed to be too pleasant, but that everything would be okay once you learned to use a tampon. It is the encounters with the harsh, but more interesting, realities of life that litter my memory of adolescence and help me make sense of my life now, in my mid twenties.

I spent the most part of my teens in Dumbarton, twelve miles along the Clyde from Glasgow. It was an industrial town built on the sweat of Irish navvies, but with the demise of the Clyde it has become a cross between a distillery town and a commuter town. Either you work in the distillery or you commute to the local nuclear bases – that is, if you have a job at all.

The assumption that life was uncomplicated was the first to go. I made my first break from childhood when I gave up horseriding. I didn't want to, but if I wanted to carry on I would have to earn some money. This meant a job, and that was the problem. The shock of mass unemployment in the 1970s reverberated in Dumbarton well into the 1980s as the main employers in the area stopped taking on apprentices, were reduced to skeleton staffs and eventually shut down. This had a drastic effect on the skilled workers in the area. Many mature men would never get a job again, many women would take up gruelling employment in the local distillery. But us lot, the young teenagers, had to deal with the prospect of *never* getting a job. (I still haven't got one ten years on.) This undermined my expectations that jobs and careers were there for the taking, and made me realise that extraneous conditions shape the course of people's lives in unavoidable ways.

Being in Dumbarton and being fourteen in the late seventies meant limited prospects. I watched my friends reject school and move into different patterns of life that didn't appeal to me. There seemed to be two options if you gave up school: either get pregnant, start a family, try for a flat in a crummy council estate and hope that your children would get a better deal in the future, or work on a soul-destroying Youth Opportunities Scheme with no money, no independence and no chance of 'getting on'. School seemed the most sensible choice to me, not through any love of learning but because I didn't want to be a mother or a yopper.

About this time, I discovered politics. My very first political activity was an anti-Thatcher rally at Blytheswood Square in 1979. Although I didn't understand why so many people were so upset about the Tories and what they stood for, it started the ball rolling. There I heard about CND and that they were setting up a branch in Dumbarton. The initial meetings were a revelation for me. I had my eyes opened to the connections between money, power and injustice in a way that I could relate to – stuck in Dumbarton with a doubtful future, surrounded by mushrooming nuclear bases.

I hadn't quite expected my future suddenly to be so bleak. I also didn't expect strangers at meetings to listen and take our opinions seriously. It was weird that our contributions didn't just meet with a wave of laughter as in school, where they thought what we said was a joke. At that time there was a lot of activity at Faslane (a nuclear depot and military submarine base) – a peace camp was set up and CND was snowballing into a national and international campaign 'just like in the '60s' – or that's what we were told by the second-time-rounders. It was an exciting time, as change seemed possible. Maybe we would be able to scupper nuclear ideals and make the world into a better place.

This uncomplicated hope did not last for long, as compromises began to surface all around the movement. It was such a disappointment when the hard edge of challenge was subordinated to the 'needs and credibility' of a national organisation. On the local level things were also getting a bit heavy with the Ministry of Defence, and local people were finding the conflicts too much. More and more people were finding employment either in the bases or as subcontractors, and this prohibited political support of CND. Because work was (and still is) so scarce, many local people had to silence their protests. These difficulties made me realise that the conflicts people had – between a livelihood and a political belief – were not easily resolved, and that life involves a certain amount of unavoidable compromise.

At this point I hit adolescence with a vengeance. Peer pressure made political activity an unacceptable and boys an acceptable focus of attention. My three pals and I became dedicated boy fanciers, started menstruating all at the same time, and had gone our separate ways by the time we were sixteen. Sex was the issue. Although we assumed that it would be with boys, there were passionate undercurrents in our relationships with each other. We were a sensual network of tangled jealousies and conflicts.

Each of us made decisions about sexuality and sex in different ways. Mine were coloured by family happenings. My elder brother left home to live with his wife and their child. Relations with my mother became distant and antagonistic. We were both fighting inner battles that allowed little room for each other, both fighting for and against our expectations of ourselves and each other. I immersed myself in the perils of peer pressure, became totally self-conscious and paranoid about boys on the outside and lavished fantasies on them inside. This paranoia was aided and abetted by my father – who made it quite clear that boys were out of bounds. Looking back, I think one of his fears was that I would get pregnant, have to get married and run the same gauntlet as my grandparents, parents, brother and best friend. So my father's prohibitions were fine by me as I realised that I couldn't handle such a situation, and it made it easier to 'wait for my hero' – who, I was convinced, would come along.

By the time I was seventeen, I was heavily into drinking and drugs. This is what you do in Dumbarton when you are a teenager. I remember great claustrophobia, and trying to block out the future – what future? I stopped reading books because all I could get my hands on were pulp romantic adventures. I had read enough of them by this time to believe in the romantic hero (I liked the dark brooding ones; pirates were best) and was depressed because mine was taking such a long time to make an appearance. I did crave other books – books which would catch my imagination and help me explore questions that I used to splurge out on paper at one in the morning. But my fantasy world was too far removed from life in Dumbarton, and so I buried it deep and became cynical about any attempt to do or change things.

Things I deemed crucial to (or maybe the point of) relationships at that time I now deeply question. This calling into question marks the start of my discovery of feminism and a lot of other things besides.

I met a guy who seemed a suitable enough antihero and decided that the time had come to 'become a woman' – i.e. lose my virginity and get a steady boyfriend(!). The trouble was – I bit off more than I could chew. I think I decided to implement my fantasies and expectations about 'what a relationship was supposed to be' on to this poor sod – he lapped it up. I demanded fidelity and constant consideration from this other person and from myself, and called it love. I did not look at another person for five years, partly because there weren't many good-looking ones about and partly because I was frightened to let go of something I had made my life in the search for maturity. Love was supposed to be for ever, and I couldn't admit to myself that I didn't like this kind of love and wasn't very happy.

After a year of going out together, I went to Glasgow University, he went to prison. Because I had immersed myself in this other person, I don't really remember much about getting to university. Studying certainly wasn't high on my agenda of activities and I didn't know anyone who had gone, either in my family or among my friends. I had managed quite successfully to deny the significance of school in my head, and going to university came as quite a shock. It was strange, new territory that didn't play a part in the 'Dumbarton world-view'. It was exciting and it was mine. My parents left me to it and supported me in many ways. They knew I was making some kind of break from their way of life, and encouraged me in this big adventure.

Even though I was lucky with such a break, living as a student brought contradictions and frustrations for me and my parents, and money was a way to voice them. Even though they had paid taxes all their working life, my parents had to pay through the nose for this 'privilege' of sending a child to university. This clashed with their assumption that education was not supposed to be a privilege any longer but a right, a right that was granted through the creation of the welfare state that had so transformed their lives (well before the time of Mrs T). Parental contribution time was tense because it took a big chunk out of their wages, and it made me financially dependent on them at a time when I was trying to assert my independence (or rather I was trying to shift my dependence from them on to my antihero).

Despite the friction and resentment caused by the cost, the hope that it would all pay off stayed because getting a degree is supposed to 'open the door' on to a secure financial future. My parents want me to be financially independent, and so do I, but the idea of securing this had to be knocked on the head. One of the hardest things to realise when you are seen as part of this idyllic student life and engulfed in the world of ideas is that there is no inherent security, especially during an economic recession and a time of political repression. A degree does not guarantee you a job, nothing does. Security based on such assumptions is very fragile, as some are finding out to their cost. These frustrations, part of student life in the eighties, echo the contradictions and difficulties faced by millions of other people.

Once at university, I still managed to block my need for learning from myself. It was something I did between prison visits. Those visits gave me ample time to experience the contradictions of 'being on the outside' – literally and in the sense of being involved with 'the socially unacceptable, criminal element'. Resentment and paranoia are a staple diet. What kind of face do you put on at a visit? Do you look the way you feel, miserable and confused, and massage his ego by not being able to manage 'with/out' him, or do you do the 'Dear John' and get on with the rest of your life, and then have the guilt of leaving someone stranded inside? There are so many questions crowding in your head in that situation. Why do it? Why me? How did I get into this situation? How do I get out? Do I ever get out? It is sad to see so many other women go through the same battles with themselves on visiting day, while you are being searched by prison officers who just see you as either cattle or scum. How much more difficult it must be when there are kids involved! I was so glad I didn't have any.

After he came out, we lived together. My resentment and paranoia never went away, although I wasn't prepared to give the relationship up. I had invested so much time and energy by now that I thought, by some weird Greek law of averages, my input would pay off and he would become the hero I wanted. It took me a long time to realise that it doesn't work like that. Being someone's conscience isn't a basis for love or friendship.

Things began to change when I was about twenty-one. My life turned somersault, and I still haven't quite sussed out what happened. I began to read feminist books for my final-year dissertation. That summer, I was stunned by the new interpretation I could put on my life. Before, I had thought I was at fault because life did not match my expectations. Now, I learned of women who were trying to question these expectations and 'failures' and explain them in terms of power, money and injustice. Thinking of things in this way explained so much more about what was going on inside my head and in the outside world. The picture fitted together more (the picture of what life is supposed to entail if you are a woman – the denial of your own desires for the sake of someone else from whom you are to draw your security – and how this dovetailed very neatly with a myriad of other rip-offs based on other simultaneous forms of oppression; for example in employment, education, opportunity, childcare and politics the world over). I could now see that the vicious circle of expectations and disappointments was not inevitable; that change was a possible and legitimate goal. I now had space inside my head to try and change my situation and expectations.

I applied for an MA in Women's Studies in Kent, and six weeks before my finals I upped and left my antihero to build a new life. This was not particularly easy. After my exams, I spent a long time chastising myself for being such a fool as to get myself into a situation that I had to run away from. It took me a long time to come to terms with 'the mistakes I had made' and accept them in a constructive way as experience that could be used to the benefit of others (hence this piece, I hope).

My sense of self was very fragile. I discovered that I had to fight myself more than anybody else, fight my old patterns of behaviour and communication, challenge my own assumptions about what I wanted and needed. I'm still not too sure of the end result because I am constantly renegotiating with myself and my desires. Some I have managed to wipe out completely, like marriage; but other, more intense personal desires are more difficult to grapple with. I still need a sense of security, love and getting on with things, but now I realise that I have to define them for myself. This is a bit of a struggle as it challenges accepted notions that are well ensconced in my head, but I prefer it this way as I have a say in the proceedings. These reformulations are important to me, and the struggle for the forms and circumstances that I find acceptable keeps me going emotionally and politically. This rebuilding of myself wouldn't have been possible without the support of those who gave me a home and caressed me while my head was going AWOL. During that unforgettable summer, I managed to find temporary work and earned enough money to go to Kent for the MA.

The MA is the next and most recent escapade. The first hurdle was finance, and the realisation that politics lies behind the allocation of funding. There is no institutional grant support now for research that is not directly linked to increased profitability. Areas of exploration that attempt to look behind the façade of 'free-market' Britain at the structures of poverty and exploitation in all forms of social relations tend to be blacklisted and starved of funds. Despite this, many people continue to think critically about the present situation and, if they are lucky enough, find a space to work on their critiques despite the pressures against them. Women's Studies sets itself up as such a space. It was the lure of such a space, coupled with a need to find out more about feminism and how it helped me change my life, the need to suss out a part of Britain that is held up as the Golden Carrot in the North, and the need to prove to myself that I could be independent financially, emotionally, and physically that made me 'head South'.

I immersed myself in academic feminism, looking for its secret. I learned that academic feminism, like everything else, is bound by the contexts of its practitioners. This is not a 'bad' thing in itself, it just means that it is very difficult to communicate across differences, even within the relative openness of an academic feminist discussion group. The impact of differences in experience and expectation was brought home by the way I was identified in the group. The act of identification was common to all, although how and what identities were used revealed a lot about our respective assumptions. The contradictions and assumptions made about me and where I come from (as my experience is the endemic example) and how these assumptions clashed with my own interpretation shed a lot of light on how the identity you give yourself is in constant motion, depending on your circumstances. I was seen as a 'white, Northern [do you mean Britain or England?] working-class girl' – a label I accepted. This brought up all sorts of contradictions about who I was, who I was supposed to be and who I wanted to be. The working-class voice was accepted under false pretences. To do this course at all meant having a degree and finding money privately to pay my fees. Both these things distanced me from what I saw as a working-class identity. I was there speaking from a position that didn't seem to fit.

Class is important, though different where I come from. Part of being Scottish is to see ourselves as both oppressed and oppressive. The Scots have been oppressed as a culture and as workers, in the past by the monarchy and now by Whitehall and its minions. Thatcherism has a lot to do with shaping the present volatile and tense cultural identity. Time and time again over the last ten years, Scotland has been used as the test bed for vicious policies. All the social security changes that reduce rights and benefits are brought in here first, in a country devastated by mass unemployment and by the erosion of the welfare state. The poll tax was implemented a full year before a revised version was imposed on the English. Despite the fact that Scotland brings in more revenue than many other parts of the country, mainly through oil, nothing is reinvested in the country's infrastructure or economy. People are not stupid, and realise that there must be some connection between this and the fact that the Scots have never supported Thatcher's government. There are only ten Tory seats for Scotland out of seventy-two such seats in Parliament at present.

The sense in which the Scots can be seen as oppressive as well as oppressed stems from the machismo within Scottish culture, and the religious intolerance and bigotry that exist between Protestants and Catholics – these oppressive elements derive also from historic conflicts over power and social control.

The complex cultural factors which lie behind any notion of a working-class identity thus made me feel profoundly uneasy with the labels that were so freely meted out at university in Kent. The assumed similarity between a variety of experiences grouped under the same name made me angry. The gulf between the two cultures was rendered invisible by the simple premiss that Scotland is part of Britain. In this way, Scotland is taken to have British cultural identity, and the template of this identity is English culture. This entanglement caused me great difficulty. How could I voice my different history, my culture's different history, when I was silenced by being assumed to be 'British'? How could I call attention to cultural diversity without sounding, instead, like a nationalist? I got confused, and retreated into theoretical speculation. A plethora of similar experiences, both on and off the course, has severely shaken my misty-eyed assumptions about academic feminism and its ability to provide solutions, its ability to resist the pressure to abstract itself from women's experience in order to be taken seriously. I have grown to respect and value the contributions of academic feminism to our understanding of difficulties we are up against, but I see their use in a limited context – in specific sites of struggle. These kinds of difficulties fascinate me on a theoretical level, but do my head in when the gulfs become real and painful.

Living in England exploded a few of my assumptions and reinforced others. Not everybody is rich, but in the South-East the wealth on show is astounding. There is a massive gulf between those who have and those who don't have access to money. Not having anything is rubbed in by the arrogant prejudice of those who can consume conspicuously. Unemployment is treated – especially in well-cushioned towns like Canterbury, where I lived – like a self-induced affliction of lazy good-for-nothings. Little do they know of the realities of an economy in recession when they are wined and dined by the vote-hungry government. After about a year I moved to London. There Thatcherism has just gone wild. Groups of people live *in* tube stations that have Rolls-Royces parked outside them. I felt like an external observer who would have to bow down to 'their' way of looking at the world if I was to belong. But, induced by visits to Glasgow, I realised that I didn't want to accept this way of life – this different, though familiar, cultural perspective. I realised that I really, really missed the people who had been part of my life before I set off on my quest, and wanted to return and re-enter the web of friendships at a different point. I decided to go back to Glasgow, carry on studying, and get involved with a feminist arts organisation. I moved up in June 1989 and smiled.

Living in such a bizarre and alien environment made me

recognise the complexity of dependence and independence. I thought that solitude meant independence, but it doesn't, it means seeing yourself as a distinct entity connected with the lives of other people. Shared experiences and shared desires are not the same as the financial and social dependence which so terrifies me. From this, I have come to realise that we all live with some notion about who we are, where we come from and where we want to go, and that these notions are rooted in where we are from, where we are, and where we want to go.

While I've been away, things have changed in Glasgow. The depression that haunted everybody's face before I left is lifting, even though life is getting tougher. The big thing at the moment is that Glasgow is 'The European City of Culture' in 1990. This is a double-edged phenomenon because the 'cultural year' can be seen as a symbol of the conflicting currents of Glasgow's identity as a European city emerging from the 1980s. Undercurrents of mistrust mingle with a buoyant hope for the future. The mistrust is based on previous experience of 'city' events. The Garden Festival turned out to be a sham because local people were not the target audience. Neither were they involved in its organisation, promotion and construction, and many were denied the privilege of seeing the flowers because of the exorbitant ticket prices. This 'sell-out' to the caprices of the precious free-market economy and consumer demands (the monied consumer) indicates that Glasgow knows how to toe the line in its self-promotion. Despite this and the rain, all is not miserable. Many people see 1990 as an opportunity to rectify this tarnished self-image and are organising in ways that challenge the current demands of 'city image'. These cross-cutting forces make Glasgow, now, a very interesting and stimulating place.

In 1990, a wide range of events is planned to highlight the history of the wealth and diversity of the city's creative talents. For people active in the arts it means access to funds for projects that 'contribute to culture'. Although Glasgow has a long history of impressive cultural and artistic production, its diversity is overshadowed by assumptions of what 'culture' is and who makes it, where it is seen as elitist artistic production by 'famous individuals' – who are predominantly men. This assumption misses the point of a plethora of creative initiatives that do not necessarily fit the mould of 'high culture'. This is a site where the demands of local people come into conflict with the absurd assumptions of present-day financial backing.

Many women who work in Glasgow are aware of these assumptions and tensions, and how they curtail their own creative production – for example, in the way they influence the allocation of exhibition space, work space and funding and concepts of what is demanded of an 'artist'. Many women do not accept this as legitimate. From this situation an umbrella organisation, Women in Profile, has developed to support women in their work and to deal with institutions that control access to work and exhibition space. Here it is the women themselves who have created this 'organisation', a space where creative energy is respected and utilised in a way which challenges the prejudices against work done by women and reflects the diversity of Glasgow's culture. It is within this context that I see myself at present as a Women in Profile participant.

It is significant that this energy has 'flourished' within a setting of cultural and artistic production. Creative, multitalented women are organising around the politics that dog the expression of creativity, in its profusion of forms at a time when 'alternative' political activity is on the increase in Scotland. Political activity is changing in that people are no longer relying on their MPs, who just want a share in governmental control, and are no longer able to organise in massive numbers (e.g. unions; and anyway, how can you unionise the unemployed?) owing to fears of government/police intervention. Feminist activity is organising itself here along different lines, in ways that have implications for feminists elsewhere and for other political struggles. These alternative routes come out of the present reality of life and opportunity and political awareness on the west coast of Scotland, and are initiatives to reformulate the means and ends of cultural production in our specific context, but in ways that establish connections with other people's contexts.

The story I have told has the backdrop of eleven years of increased oppression, repression and depression under a Thatcherite government. I realise that there are millions of people struggling to survive in this and harsher regimes. I have tried to stress that personal experiences and strategies are linked together through networks of family, friends and shared struggles, and want to say that for me, these networks can and do serve as the ground from which to work to change things. These networks are the link between experience and political change. Personal experiences change the way we react to the world, and it is these feelings and understandings that 'guide' the desire to act – to be political – to be ourselves.

13
Fighting the Red Wolf

Valerie Malcolm

I am a young Black woman now studying Applied Social Studies with Social Work at Bradford University. At the start of the 1980s I was ten.

I have Systemic Lupus Erythmatosus (SLE). This was diagnosed when I was about thirteen. The name, translated, means something like 'the red wolf of the system'. This apparently arose because of the red facial rash which can occur and was said to look like the attack of a wolf. SLE is an autoimmune disease. The body forms antibodies which act against itself. These antibodies circulate in the blood and can attack any blood vessel, which causes inflammation. Any organ in the body can be affected by this, so the lupus sufferer can have complaints ranging from skin rashes and general tiredness to arthritis, kidney or heart trouble. The disease follows a pattern of flares of activity and periods of remission, with good days and bad days in between. The disease mostly affects women of childbearing age. The cause of SLE is still unknown, although the tendency to get it is higher if another family member has the disease.

I was introduced to the NHS in the early eighties because of the disease. When my first large lupus flare took me into hospital, I found it an exciting place. As the flares continued as I got older, the thought of going back into hospital became a less and less exciting prospect. Stress can bring on a flare, so exam times at school were difficult for me. I had a lot of support from school friends and teachers – and the family, who put up with moods and tears and gave me a lot of encouragement. My sister Beryl was a great strength, carrying my books – and me sometimes – to and from school, and collecting work when I was unwell.

I have also gained a lot of strength and support from my Christian faith and my local Methodist church in London in the past. The members of the church are very warm and welcoming people and are still very supportive now, although I don't attend church very often. They counselled me and visited me when I was in hospital, and they have given me financial help. After my last visit to hospital they helped me to buy the drugs I needed because I hadn't yet got free prescriptions.

I am not the active Christian I was. I have some problems with Christianity, which I am trying to resolve, and I have stepped back a little from the Church. When I was at school, I found it difficult to believe that my friends from other faiths would not reach heaven. After a lot of thought and discussion I decided that there were many paths which could be followed to reach God.

More recently I have had problems with the faith in three different areas, which I'll go into briefly. I've learnt more history relevant to me in these last years, and have been shocked by the way the Christian faith has been used to oppress people, to destroy their cultures and their lives. My ancestors were treated in this way, and people are still being hurt today. I find it hard to connect what I believe with this faith. I also disagree with the belief within Christianity that you are in some way evil if you are lesbian or gay. People should have the right to determine their own sexuality, and should not be condemned for it. I have problems too with the role of women in the Church – that women are in some way less important in God's eyes and have a less important part to play. This has been difficult for me to work through within the Church, and I suppose I feel more distant from it now because of this. But I still believe in God, and I am sure s/he believes in me.

Lupus was rarely diagnosed when my mother started to get migraines and painful joints. The pain would keep her from work for a day or two and then go. She never looked ill. Mum got her first diagnosis in the sixties in Cambridge. She was told she was suffering from a 'tropical disease' – she was Black – which was affecting her eyes, and could cause blindness. The new drug prescribed for her caused sickness, and it was stopped. The 'tropical disease' did not worsen – or cause blindness. So when my parents planned to move to London, Mum was discharged with no further treatment planned. The pain, however, wouldn't stay away, and after many visits to the GP and for tests, she was referred to the Hammersmith Hospital. The doctors in the rheumatology team there finally put a name to the disease. Although not that much was known about this disease, it was a relief to know its name.

My mother's attitude towards the disease has influenced mine. Despite being quite ill at times – once spending six months in hospital – she has refused to let the disease take over her life. She would try to keep going during bad days, not sitting down until she had to, to shake the pain off. She has a lot of strength. She has a strong dislike of hospitals and the drugs and their side-effects, and decided to live without them, reducing the treatment gradually herself. Her views have often led to disagreements with my doctors. On one occasion when I was quite ill she discharged me from hospital for what she was certain was better treatment at home: her treatment worked. Her attitude has challenged me. I would also like to do without the doctors and the drugs, but this has been a difficult goal for me to achieve so far. The disease has been going through an active period and I don't feel that I can take chances with my body at the moment. In the future, when the disease activity is at a low stage, I would like to find an alternative treatment to control the SLE. I've heard that you can now find alternative medicine on the NHS and I'd like to discover more about this.

I find the hospital system – the clinics and the wards – confusing and frustrating. My last stay in hospital brought some of my thoughts together more clearly. I felt the need to be treated as a person, not just as the SLE case in bed 10. There should be time to treat the person as a whole. This means listening to a woman's feelings about her body, the pain and the treatment – and not just dealing with a particular part of the body. Patients should be given as much information as they need to help them understand what's happening in their bodies. This time I made myself ask 'Why?' repeatedly when I was told something – and said 'No' to all tests and drugs until the need for them and the side-effects were explained in detail. I found it was the only way to get the information I required about my body. I found it very intimidating being a small Black woman with a quiet voice, trying to keep strong in front of tall white men in white coats – calling me a 'sensible girl'.

SLE is a confusing disease. Here I am striving for a sense of wholeness while my body is destroying itself. This body I value sometimes tries to self-destruct, and I can't understand or control it. Sometimes I think I fight the doctors because I must fight, and I can't fight myself.

Although I wasn't particularly concerned with the state of the health service when I was first admitted at thirteen, I found my last visit worrying. I had not been in hospital for three years and I could see some of the effects of the cuts the Thatcher government has made to the NHS. Half the ward I was put on was closed because of a lack of staff and resources. However, the twelve beds that were available were never empty for long – new patients were moved in within hours of others leaving. The demand was there, but not the money. Equipment was broken; some was borrowed from another ward. I had forgotten to bring a towel – the ward didn't have any to spare.

The cleaning and catering in the hospital are now carried out by private contractors. In my first week there, our cleaner was covering two wards – an impossible task. There were complaints about every meal; the letters of complaint to the caterer went unanswered while I was there. Patients were going to the staff canteen for meals, or asking their families to bring in some food. The hospital staff were trying to make people well under these conditions.

This was my experience of just one ward, but it was a worrying experience and certainly not an isolated case. The whole health system is in need of resources that the government is not prepared to provide. With poor equipment and low morale it becomes almost impossible to give the patient the care they require. I have mixed feelings about my own doctors and drugs – but I probably wouldn't be alive without the NHS, so I'm grateful for it and I find the government's actions and its future plans in the new White Paper very disturbing. We all need to do what we can to protect the health service. I can only see a better future for the NHS without the Thatcher government.

Although I am now doing social work, I took science subjects at school. The school had a quick turnover of staff, and I was lucky to find four young women teachers there who were a great inspiration to me. Two of them were my science teachers. They all showed me a new way of thinking. I was introduced to the concept of equal opportunities for women, and to feminism. They brought refreshing views into the classroom and taught me a lot outside class as well. They helped me to develop my ideas and encouraged me to aim for the course in Bradford. I still see these women today, though not as often as I would like.

I am now in the third year of this four-year course, and I

am currently on a placement in an area office in Bradford for three months. Although the course is not brilliant, I really like living in Bradford and studying there. I have met some good people here and in London in the last three years, and have made some important friends. I have also learnt a lot about myself here. I started to read literature by Black women and about Black women in Bradford, and was introduced to Black feminism. I have learnt a lot from my sister Beryl, who studies in nearby Sheffield, and from Kum Kum Bhavnani, the lecturer who suggested that I write this piece. I joined the Women's Group in Bradford and organised the women's self-defence group for a short while, but I found the Black Women's Group has given me the most pleasure.

The Black Women's Group ran for one year, last year. The atmosphere was brilliant – it was a mixture between a discussion group, a support group and a general meeting-place. There was a lot of lively and interesting discussion. Our discussions on our experiences in the education system proved how difficult it still is for Black women to get through the system even today, but also showed that people would not give up fighting, in spite of the barriers. Many of the women in the group left university at the end of the year, and it has not been organised again since then, but I hope it will come together again in the future.

The Black Women's Group made me think about how isolated I was from the Black community in Bradford, by just being in the student community. So this year I enrolled in an assertiveness class for Black women in Bradford, but I have had to miss classes so far because of being ill with kidney trouble. I will find a way of doing it, even if I have to enrol again. I also started work in a Saturday school for Black kids before Christmas and want to continue with that.

As for the future – I have said before that the future for the NHS would be a better one without the Conservative government. That's something we must all secure, along with a better future for the country as a whole in the next election.

More personally I am looking forward to the 1990s. I am coming to accept SLE as part of my life for the moment, although like my mother I want to control it and beat it in the future in my own way, and gain the sense of wholeness I'm striving for. There are interesting and dramatic changes happening in the world around me – for example the revolutions taking place in Eastern Europe. And in South Africa the release of Nelson Mandela – that's very exciting, but there's a long, long way to go before apartheid is ended. I want to see and be part of these changes. The new decade gives me hope for a new way of living.

I came to know Valerie Malcolm during her time as a student in the Department of Applied Social Studies at the University of Bradford. When I first mentioned the possibility of a Black women's group in the University, Valerie was very excited, and urged me to get on with organising it. I am so glad I did. She confided in me how much she wanted a placement with a Black organisation, and asked for my advice on how best to approach the appropriate tutors. She also informed me that she was not pleased when I told her I would be in the USA for twelve months, until August 1990. But we had agreed to discuss her placements, her future jobs and what had been happening in the Black women's group when I returned – when she would be in her final year.

Valerie was quiet but she was not shy, and was often direct. She never hesitated to voice her opinions to me. Her strength during periods of intense pain, her determination to speak out against poverty, racism and gendered inequalities, as well as her joy at being with women whenever possible – both black and white – are some of the clearest memories I have of her. Her acute sense of humour was also very much a part of the persona many of us were lucky to see.

All these qualities are central in much of what is being forged in the name of feminism by women of Valerie's generation. I respect and admire these qualities – as I respected and admired Valerie.

Valerie died in March 1990.

Kum-Kum Bhavnani
Oberlin College, Ohio, USA,
May 1990

14
A 'Pretended' Family

Chris Pegg

Recently I asked my mother and grandmother to write their autobiographies; the result made me think about my sense of background and my idea about families, my family in particular. There are certain things I have in common with my mother and grandmother – we are all white women born and raised in the English Midlands, all of us know how to make do in lean times, we are all regarded by the rest of our family as talkers, as good cooks and as strong-minded women likely to speak our minds and get our own way. Also, we are all mothers of daughters and we all have first-born girl children. There the similarities stop. My mother is and my grandmother was married: I am not. More importantly, perhaps – in this climate of institutionalised homophobia, encouraged by Clause 28 – not only am I an unmarried mother but a lesbian mother too.

Both my grandmother and mother have spent the greater part of their adult lives devoted to marriage and motherhood, undertaking the responsibilities of men and children; although both have also undertaken paid work and my mother has had a steady job for years. I don't intend to spend any of my adult life in this way; my notions of the responsibilities of motherhood are vastly different from theirs and don't involve any idea of self-sacrifice. None of us 'planned' our children, but the consequences of unplanned motherhood have been different in each case. (My grandmother had two children, six years apart – both 'in wedlock' and both now married with families of their own. My mother had three children, four and six years apart, also within her marriage; I have one child and don't intend to have any more.) We all love our children in our various ways, although I suspect our definitions of such love would be very different; and we all love one another, although our relationships are neither easy nor problem-free because of our many differences, not least of which is the fact that my grandmother is a Christian while my mother and I are not.

One of the things that has changed a great deal since my grandmother's youth is that not only is abortion legal and available (to some) free on the NHS, but it is much easier than it used to be to bring up a child outside marriage (either the legal type or 'common-law'). Much of the stigma for those of us who used to be called unmarried mothers and are now more generally referred to as single parents has gone, although the financial and emotional hardships remain almost unchanged.

My grandmother's autobiography is mainly about her childhood in a poor family of thirteen children, the Second World War, and her married life to my grandfather, who died six years ago and whom she adored. Because she was a girl in such a large family my grandmother's early life was one of drudgery and strict discipline. She remains a strict disciplinarian herself – 'If a job's worth doing, it's worth doing well', she says, and insists on this; I remember as a child being made to do chores over again if they were not done to her satisfaction.

She is a formidable lady, my grandmother, capable of making moral judgements based on how clean the milk bottles on people's doorsteps are. During the war she kept rabbits in order to supplement her family's rations, but could never face killing them. My mother is less of a disciplinarian although they share the same strong sense that some things are 'not nice'. She has made less of a career out of her marriage and child-raising, taking her job (as a swimming teacher) as seriously as her domestic work. Her autobiography is longer than my grandmother's and closer to mine, as she grew up in less poverty than her mother and came from a smaller family.

She tells a good story, does my mother, such as the 'Yorkshire Pudding Story': in her first year of marriage to my dad my mother had a great deal of trouble with the cooking, and especially with the cooking of Yorkshire pudding. One Sunday, while my dad was out fishing, she'd spent the whole morning cooking the Sunday dinner plus the 'offering' of Yorkshire pud, and over dinner came the famous words 'This Yorkshire pudding doesn't taste like the ones my mother used to make.' My mother opened the back door in despair and rage to throw the offending pudding out to the birds when the back door of the house next door flew open and a voice shouted: 'I don't even like Yorkshire pudding!' and over the dividing fence sailed – yes, a Yorkshire pudding. I have this vision of women all over Derbyshire hurling Yorkshire puddings over fences of a Sunday dinner time!

My mother's sense of family is strong, as strong as my grandmother's. 'Blood is thicker than water' they say, and they mean it too. The women in my family have always helped each other out, especially in the first year of a new baby, in a variety of ways – washing, cooking, housework, childminding, gifts of clothes or furniture, sympathy and support. There is a sense in which we look after each other, although this is by no means unconditional support, and criticism is offered often enough along with the assistance. I have benefited from such help in many ways – in fact I'd never have made it to university without it. The amount of unpaid childcare and material assistance in the form of winter shoes and coats that I've had from my family over the years has enabled me to pursue my own interests and get a degree (unheard of in the women of our family until my generation).

Since the last Women's Liberation Conference in Britain in 1978 (when I was fifteen and busy bunking off school, learning to inhale cigarette smoke without coughing, and other such important aspects of life) there have been a lot of changes. A number of women have gatecrashed the professions and 'made it' into management, 'women's culture' has become institutionalised within the capitalist system – with companies such as Virago actually making money out of it – and everything from trekking in Nepal to writing weekends in Wiltshire exclusively in the company of one's sisters is on offer in the back pages of *Spare Rib*.

We've had the Equal Opportunities Act, and Thatcher's notion of individualism and achievement apparently applies to women as well as men – in theory. Thatcherism doesn't make special provision for women because its ideology encompasses the notion that it is no longer necessary; the liberal feminist idea of 'equality' is supposed to have been achieved; thus things like increasing child benefit are regarded as silly – presupposing that women will only have to pay it back in tax anyway! The notion of 'post-feminism' is bandied about – surely British women are emancipated and liberated by now, and there's a condom machine in every pub loo to prove it!

Meanwhile 'Women's Liberation' as an organised (inter)national movement no longer exists, but feminism is all-pervasive. Many gains have been made, especially in terms of putting the experiences of a diversity of women – working-class women, Black women, lesbians and women with disabilities – on the 'women's agenda', and getting away from the white middle-class bias of 1970s feminism. Some examples of this have been the rethinking of demands like 'a woman's right to choose' and 'abortion on demand' in class/race terms, and campaigns around 'reproductive rights' which include the right to have children for those women who are discouraged or prevented by the state, as well as the right not to have children. Nevertheless, childcare remains largely a private, and often a lonely, affair, as does the domain of 'the family'.

I was sixteen years old in 1979, and at school in Derby, where I intended to stay and do A levels (I didn't want to take a typing course or work in a bank, which was what girls seemed to do if they left school at sixteen; I was in fact quite bright, although I didn't know it). I don't know what I wanted from life in those days – nothing more than a good time, I think. I was a slow developer intellectually and had little sense of myself as distinct from anything else. I had a boyfriend, I'd had several before (plus a 'girlfriend' and several crushes which I had so far managed to ignore the implications of). He said he loved me, I said I loved him, we used to fuck in his father's study under cover of listening to music. I never enjoyed it much, it hadn't occurred to me I could – it was what you did with boys! I remember arguing against the sexual double standard at school and defending my right to 'sleep with whoever I liked' (never realising that had I really examined this notion I would be sleeping with the blonde sixth-former who made my stomach churn when I saw her and who ate most of my sandwiches at lunch time).

O levels loomed and I felt sick at the thought. I hadn't paid much attention to school work since my girls' grammar went comprehensive in 1976 and discipline slipped. Pottery I adored, and English literature (although both my grammar and spelling were appalling); the rest I ignored as much as possible, and I skived off as often as I dared. I tried to organise my revision, but I still felt sick until it dawned on me that this wasn't nerves! Pregnancy wasn't something I'd thought about, and no plans for the future had included motherhood since the age of about five. I told my boyfriend; he was delighted for an instant, then serious – what was I going to do? What was he going to say to his parents (who were very 'respectable' and, worse still, Methodists)? I said I didn't know but I thought I wanted this baby. Later, after seeing the doctor and an agonising ten-day wait for the result of the test (I already knew), the implications hit me; also, I would have to tell *my* parents.

In the end I didn't have to do this as my mother found out; she had a way of doing this which included reading my diaries. There was a huge scene during which she said she wouldn't tell my father if I had an abortion – I walked out. Staying at a friend's house for a few days we talked it over; all four of my close friends were adamant that I should have an abortion. 'What about adoption?' I argued, not much liking the idea, but in the end I decided on abortion, much to my boyfriend's relief when I told him later; now no one would have to know.

After my O levels my parents went on holiday with my younger brother and sister, and I went into hospital and had an abortion. No one knew, so no one came to see me for days. I developed an infection, couldn't stop crying and was desperate to go home. Eventually my boyfriend managed to sneak in a visit and arranged for a friend of his to come and fetch me home the next day, but the minute I got there my temperature rocketed and I was delirious for about a week.

My parents rang and insisted we joined them on holiday. I managed to drag myself down, but I felt terrible. I told no one how I felt but cried a lot, in secret if possible – stopping when people got near. My boyfriend and I then went to see Led Zeppelin at Knebworth Park; when we got back he started his job. My parents were away all summer and so, it seemed, were most of my friends. I don't remember doing much besides crying, although when my O level results came through I was relieved to find that I'd managed to pass four of them (everyone, including me, thought I'd fail the lot). By the end of that summer I'd lost so much weight that I was only six and a half stone!

In September I went back to school, into the sixth form, and spent as much time as possible in the pottery studio. I decided that I'd do a degree in ceramics (for which I knew I'd have to do a year's foundation course at the local 'tec', but I was prepared to stick this out) and worked towards that. I didn't talk much, and after a brief but disastrous engagement to my 'steady' at Easter 1980 I slept around a great deal. Then I started having stomach pain, and after repeatedly visiting the doctor and being told that there was nothing wrong with me and it was probably psychosomatic guilt from my abortion, I was finally sent to a specialist. I seemed to spend a great deal of 1980 having tests, and I spent my eighteenth birthday in hospital – I had a cyst on my ovary. All the time I was ill I read everything I could get my hands on, including Firestone's *The Dialectic of Sex*, which I picked up at a jumble sale, because I thought it was about sex, but which I got into even when I found it wasn't. This was the first 'feminist' book I ever read, and it had a profound effect on me.

Then came 1981 and my A levels. I wasn't sure about this university business; no one in my family apart from one cousin had ever done such a thing, but as I was regarded as 'arty' it seemed okay. I had an interview at the 'tec' and got a place on the foundation course, I was resitting my maths O level, all seemed in order – then I discovered that I was pregnant again!

With the amount of screwing around I did it was only a matter of time before this happened; I had gone on the Pill after my abortion, but it gave me headaches and made me feel bad and eventually I just stopped taking it. I still went to the clinic and collected the prescriptions but I didn't swallow the stuff any more. This time I told nobody, sat my A levels and threw up in the mornings. Finally I told my pottery teacher that I wasn't going to college because I was going to have a baby – so, I had decided! (I'd waited till it was past four months anyway, so it was too late to have an abortion, I wasn't going through that again.) Then I told some of my friends. How was I going to tell my mother? At that point my mother had a sprained ankle and was laid up with it; one morning I took her breakfast up and she said, 'Isn't there something you think you ought to tell me?' (or words to that effect) and I told her I was pregnant, that I was going to have this baby on my own, and that there was nothing she could do to stop me. That was that hurdle over!

I lost a few friends but most rallied round, as did some of my mother's who gave me second-hand baby clothes. My father stopped speaking to me, as did the bloke concerned (whom I'd told but made it clear that I wanted nothing from him), my mother tried to 'make the best of things'. I was working at two part-time jobs I'd had for ages but had to give them up, the kitchen job was making me feel sicker than I already was, and who ever heard of a pregnant pool attendant? I began my long acquaintance with social security forms, questions, more forms, and lots of queueing, taking up more and more space in the queues as my pregnancy advanced over the summer and autumn of 1981.

I hated every minute of being pregnant. I felt sick all the time, in the early stages I threw up a lot, I couldn't bear the smell of cigarette smoke after about five months, suffered from cramp and heartburn and was generally depressed. Mainly I lay on my bed and stared at the ceiling, although I still went out from time to time, but I hated being so big and heavy and felt I stuck out a mile in pubs and clubs. I read every childcare and childbirth book in the library; I even bought one from Mothercare! All of them assumed that pregnant women were married/partnered, happy, well off and regarded the birth of their babies as the start of a 'family'; this made me even more depressed – what about women like me?

The last two months were the worst. I was uncomfortable all the time and miserable as hell; all I wanted was to get 'it' over with. My father still wasn't speaking to me in any significant manner (not that I noticed the difference much, apart from the lack of derogatory remarks). Being in the house so much with my mother, who was at that point working evenings, had meant that we'd done some talking, but I was adamant that I wanted to give birth alone and refused all offers of company, including hers. So on December 15th, at about six o'clock in the evening, I walked up the road to the waiting ambulance (we were snowed in) and got in it alone.

What followed is not an experience I want to repeat. I'd read the technical details of labour a million times, although I couldn't face going to classes. I was scared stiff, which couldn't have helped, and horrified by the 'conveyor-belt' feel of hospital birth. Still, by 7.45 the next morning I was delivered of a baby girl, and although torn, exhausted, and a bit tearful, I was overwhelmed with joy.

I'd read about postnatal depression: three out of five women get it and I fully expected to be one of them; instead I came alive. Not that it wasn't difficult, it was, and I was always tired and sometimes I despaired; but I thrived on the challenge of asserting myself as a single mother, I felt better than I had ever felt since my abortion. At first I lived with my parents but when my daughter was nine months old I got a council house (after being on the waiting list for fourteen months). It was on the other side of town from my parents (exactly the same estate as my dad grew up on, by coincidence, and not far from where my grandparents still lived). Here I 'sorted myself out' – my plan was to stay at home with my daughter until she went to school (I'd absorbed all kinds of ideas about 'good motherhood' without realising it) and then go to college as I had originally planned.

I got involved on the edges of CND activities, although I never actually joined CND and I was too scared to do 'direct action' because I was worried about what would happen to the baby if I got arrested. I heard about Greenham and knew people who had been, but it was action around Molesworth that I got involved with, which was a mixed protest. I had various people to stay as I had the space to put them up; some of them (of whom I was secretly in awe) were at university in London; among them were women who called themselves feminists. At first they intimidated me, they seemed so sure of themselves, then I came to think of them as allies – one woman in particular, who has remained a close friend over the years, giving generously of both personal and political support.

So September 1982 found me living alone with my daughter. I did feel very isolated sometimes; none of my friends had children, which seemed to make a world of difference between me and them. I got bad agoraphobia from time to time, particularly if my mother had the baby (who wasn't really a baby any more). With the pushchair in front of me I felt capable of anything! I drank fairly heavily in the evenings in order not to think too much about how I felt.

At Christmas I had to have another small operation as the scar from the last one had become reinfected. I drank more after that and began to find 'devoting myself' to my daughter more and more difficult, and by the time she was sixteen months old I could hardly manage more than the basics of feeding, washing and dressing her, cooking, shopping and cleaning. Playing around with her and chatting (more listening, since she learned to speak), which had been such a pleasure, now seemed to drain all my energy. I longed to hear an adult voice in the evenings and would let just about anyone into the house. I talked too much, too fast and too loud in company, but I couldn't help it.

In the summer of 1983 I joined a toy library a woman in the park had told me about; it was hard at first as my daughter wasn't used to other children and behaved quite aggressively towards them, but everyone was very understanding about it and she soon stopped and began to play with only the usual amount of squabbling among small children. After a while I began to work for the community centre that ran it, mainly running a crèche for their 'drop-in advice service' and helping with the toy library. I met other women who were mothers, single or married, whom I could talk to; we had a great deal in common – isolation, poverty, frustration at the kids, anxiety and tiredness, often a feeling of not being able to cope. I felt much better knowing other women felt the same way, less abnormal. A friend gave me *Of Woman Born* by Adrienne Rich, and the analysis of the 'institution of motherhood' made perfect sense. It wasn't children themselves that were a problem but the way 'motherhood' is constructed by a society which puts all the responsibility on one woman and holds her accountable for any 'mistakes'. I wasn't describing myself as a feminist at that point, but was getting a reputation for being stroppy.

In autumn 1983 I went to college, with encouragement from the community centre people, to do a mature students' course and get some decent A levels (plus maths O level, which I still hadn't managed to pass). To do this I found a childminder to whom I shall always be grateful and whom I paid the paltry sum of 80p an hour! Even so my bill came to £12 a week, which was a large chunk out of my social security! But I was determined and managed somehow. It was at college that my politics began to crystallise. It was only a small college and there were no radical actions (this was '83, not '68, after all) or demos or whatnot, but I and one or two other women did our own informal 'consciousness raising' and that truly radicalised my life. Through this talking I found that many of our problems were shared. Although the father of my daughter had never been around and anyone else was incidental to her for years, I was still sleeping with men at that point. I made yet more connections about why I felt things; how, as a single mother and as a woman, I was forced into certain patterns of life/behaviour, certain things were expected of me that I found impossible.

I got formally introduced to feminism at college, and was lucky enough to have a wonderful teacher who had been a sixties radical and encouraged us all to question things. This had a very great influence on me, particularly reading books such as Ann Oakley's *Housewife*. There was a lot of support on that course and I was so eager to learn that I read and read and studied every spare minute I got. I worked late into the night when my daughter was safely in bed, I fell asleep over my books, it all seemed so *important* somehow. I never stopped talking in or out of class; my head was reeling. I also discovered something I hadn't known before – I was intelligent and people, amazingly, seemed to listen and be interested in what I said.

I got an A in my A level sociology and even passed my maths (just). Now what? I was too scared to go to university as my friends from the course were doing; my daughter was only two and a half and I felt part of a community somehow. There were lots of single mothers where I lived and some of us had begun to talk to each other and help each other out. The toy library was going very well; my daughter had learnt to relate to other children after a shaky start and seemed happier for it. She loved her time at the childminder's and the other children there as well as the kids at the toy library. I had my London University friends as well as my older Derby friends. I was consciously reading 'feminist' books and making changes. I became more confident and enjoyed living alone with my daughter, relating to her more easily now she wasn't the only thing in my life. My drinking eased a little and became less desperate. The only blot on the horizon that summer was that my grandfather was dying of cancer.

In the autumn I felt a bit at a loss as both my close friends from college had gone to Keele to do degrees. I did another year and another A level to fill time. 1984 was less intense emotionally, although I still worked maniacally hard and got another A. I was much more definite about my feminism now, but much less definite about my sexuality, finding relationships with men more and more problematic. Lesbianism and feminism I hadn't really connected until one of my feminist friends 'came out' that year and we talked about sexuality a lot. I was unhappy with my current relationship (with a man) and began to think through why this was so. Now I had a new plan: I would move away from Derby and go to university and study sociology rather than ceramics, as I had originally intended.

In September 1985 I left family and friends behind and moved into family accommodation on the campus of Sussex University, which is the smallest space I have ever lived in, although it is surrounded by fields and trees. My daughter went to the nursery there three and a half days a week, which was bliss; my last year of college I'd been using a combination of childminder, play group and two afternoons in a nursery the other side of town, with back-up from my mother and an enlisted friend for dropping her off and picking her up (to cover the time I had to be in the college and time to study) and had seemed to spend a great deal of time on my bike taking her to and fetching her from various places.

University life suited us both. She had more freedom to roam than on an estate near a main road, and a bunch of kids of all ages and from all over the place to play with – she took to it like a duck to water and didn't seem to miss anyone. I met a whole load of new people: other single parents, women who had been struggling to get 'an education', feminists, lesbians, radicals and politicos of various sorts. I joined the Women's Group and went on several demos – mainly local things over student issues.

Going to university had been what I'd been aiming at for such a long time that I could hardly believe I'd made it. Babysitting was a bit of a problem at first – I missed my mother's support for this but I soon got to know people and it became easier. I felt very unsure of myself to start off with and living down South was a bit of a culture shock. I felt very 'unsophisticated' and 'uncultured' compared to the other students but got over this after a while, although I was always delighted to bump into another Northerner. I worked really hard and enjoyed every minute of it, and spent my evenings socialising with the other mature students living on campus. We used to do a lot of things communally and the photos I have from the summer of '86 make the whole set-up look idyllic. Reality was, as always, more complicated than this and there were problems enough, not least with the accommodation, which was in a bad way. There was a real sense of all being in it together, though, and the women in particular gave each other a lot of help (especially at crisis points, of which there were many due to the financial and emotional strain most of us were living under).

By my second year I was part of the 'women's collective' within the students' union, trying to organise events for the Women's Group and so forth. I participated in the picket of *Nine and a Half Weeks* at the local cinema, which sparked off a debate over pornography and censorship in the pages of *Spare Rib* and elsewhere. There wasn't masses of feminist action, however, and my politics were still shaped much more by informal talking with women (and a few men) in bars or at my flat when my daughter was asleep than by 'organised feminism'. I did discover the 'women's scene' socially, though, which made a lot of difference.

In the second term of my second year I 'came out' as a lesbian, which was easier in a university environment than it would have been in many other places (it took me another five months to summon up the courage to tell my mum, though not until June '87 did I manage it. Her reaction was much better than I'd expected). Coming out around my daughter wasn't easy; I knew the possible implications of public lesbian motherhood although I'm never likely to have problems over custody. I wasn't worried about how it would affect her on campus as it was one difference among many, but was worried about how it might affect her at school. Admitting to being a lesbian *mother* was very problematic.

In my third year I mainly worked maniacally to get everything done in time and found time for only a bit of political action – demos mainly, over the Alton Bill and Clause 28, and also Lesbian Strength and Gay Pride marches on which I felt very much a newcomer. Then in '88 I graduated with an upper second and got a job cleaning on the university campus for the summer, at the end of which I moved into town to share a house with a friend of mine who's also a single parent. I still live in this household of five, two of whom are kids, which I feel to be a solid base for both me and my daughter.

Things like the Women's Centre, lesbian line, the local Stop the Clause campaign, and the rest of the women's community, both political and social, which I now take for granted as part of my everyday life, I would have found impossible to imagine ten years ago. Both my daughter and I have written articles for the local lesbian and gay magazine *A Queer Tribe* and she is comfortable with the idea that her mother is a lesbian, although old enough to understand that not everyone else is!

I'm still studying, although part-time now, and at Kent University, not Sussex, and my ambition is eventually to get a PhD. Meanwhile I'm still on social security and I still have problems with childcare. I can't afford enough of it or to get a full-time job because of how much full-time childcare would cost and the organisational hassle; although I get a lot of informal unpaid support from various people there always seem to be snags of one kind or another. Living in a place that has an established women's community, as well as being regarded as 'the lesbian capital of the South', has made many things much easier for me. As my daughter is growing up in a 'pretended family relationship' which the state wants to abolish and even deny, the presence of a lesbian and gay community is a constant comfort. Brighton has a lot of women's events, courses and so on, which I enjoy; they seem to be one of the benefits of the last ten years of feminist struggle.

In the seventies came the notion that 'just' motherhood wasn't enough for many women; with books such as Friedan's *The Feminine Mystique* came the suggestion that (heterosexual) women 'add' a job to marriage and motherhood in order to gain fulfilment. Motherhood itself still remains an individual concern in the eighties despite a quantity of political, fictional, and therapeutic writing on the mother–daughter relationship. Many of us still 'choose' to undertake it, and with AID it has become easier for lesbian couples to have children. Even in the era of the 'New Man' it is still largely women who raise kids, and this hasn't changed significantly over the last ten years. Much of the conflict I've had has been over trying to be a mother and a person at the same time, and although I love my daughter dearly and can't imagine life without her I sometimes wish the responsibility for her wasn't mine (or at least not mine alone).

Looking back over the last ten years, for eight of which I have been a mother, it's difficult to get a grasp on who I was then. I was no less a 'feminist' in 1979 than I am now; it's just that I'd never heard the word. In ten years I've come a long way – nearly three hundred miles geographically from North to South, and to a self-acceptance as a lesbian and an adequate mother, with a politics into which I can fit my personal beliefs. However, it's difficult not to censure, to gloss over stupid mistakes and very painful episodes, to reject parts of myself because they're not very 'right-on', or refuse to look at the implications of others. Much has changed for me in the past decade, yet much remains the same. I get the sense of having come a long way but of struggles not being at an end, either personally or in terms of feminist work, and much hard graft still to come.

It has taken a long time and a great deal of effort for me to get where I am, but I don't mean the autobiographical aspect of my writing here as a 'confession' so much as a way of looking at a decade in which feminism has changed a great deal, and at the personal landscape which has made me who I am and influenced the way I feel about that feminism.

15

So Who's Next in the Firing Line?

Clare Ramsaran

My personal version of the eighties began with covering my classroom walls with 'Who killed Blair Peach?' posters. These were torn down, funnily enough, by my classmates before the teachers even got to them. However, when I gave them some Anti-Nazi League literature which featured Johnny Rotten they soon switched their allegiances from the National Front to the ANL. In retrospect I realise that this was a musical rather than a political choice.

At the time my thirteen-year-old logic allowed me to reconcile being a member of both the Catholic Church and School Kids Against the Nazis (the youth branch of the ANL).

I remember going on my first march, which was an ANL one. My dad was supposed to be taking me – during an access visit – but he'd forgotten he was supposed to be seeing me and had arranged to work. I was really annoyed and humiliated when he dropped me off at the march and then asked a steward to keep an eye on me. However, I soon made friends with some other kids (also lefty teenagers) and had a great time. I found it a very exciting and powerful feeling being on a march like that, and it made it all worthwhile to be part of a group of like-minded people.

It wasn't until I was older that I learned about internal politicking and how in politics most of your fighting is done with your allies rather than your enemies. As a young teenager I was oblivious to this and ready to change the world.

Having followed my older sister into the ANL, it wasn't too long before I followed her into feminism. She casually left copies of *Spare Rib* around the house which I picked up and read. I became convinced that patriarchy would collapse if only we had women priests. I remember having a heated argument with my Guide leader (a nun) on this issue. Needless to say, this got me nowhere fast and I soon embraced a new-found atheism.

At the time I was unwillingly attending a Catholic girls' school and living in Isleworth, a nondescript suburb in the West London Borough of Hounslow. Hounslow consisted of a high street, several tube stations, a barracks and plenty of houses in between. Being on the flight path to Heathrow provided a noisy reminder, every few minutes, of our proximity to the airport.

By 1982 I was eager to leave school, and had decided to be an engineer. This was not exactly encouraged in my school, which wanted us to be good Catholic wives and mothers, or career women (or preferably both). I started applying for apprenticeships and eagerly attended a careers talk by British Airways at school, hoping to find out about getting an apprenticeship with BA. In my naive optimism I had failed to realise that the careers talk was on 'How to become an air hostess' – which wasn't quite my intention. I knew engineering wasn't the done thing – not really a girls' subject – but I wasn't going to let that stop me – in fact it probably spurred me on.

But when the intention threatened to become a reality and I was asked to go for aptitude tests, offered provisional places, etc., I suffered a crisis of confidence and dropped the whole thing. I didn't think I could face however many years of being watched for every little mistake, just to prove that women really *were* inferior. So I opted for the more feminine A levels at my local college.

Meanwhile, other things were happening in the big wide world. Various events were taking place in Britain and internationally during the ten years which were collectively to become known as the eighties.

As the decade drew to a close, it was time for all the colour supplements and TV current affairs programmes to do their reviews of the eighties. Watching these reviews, and seeing all the photos and news footage from the past ten years, made me realise how easy it is to forget fairly recent major events. I found myself thinking nostalgically, 'Oh yes, I remember the Falklands', as if I was some sort of World War II veteran.

After seeing these various versions of the eighties, I was left mainly with images of confrontation in one form or another: the Falklands, the riots, the miners' strike, Broadwater Farm – the list goes on.

These events had faded in my memory and I found it hard to believe that they had happened so recently. This is partly due to the way news is presented in such an oversimplified way. TV news especially tended to characterise events in terms of a single image – such as the classic riots footage of a young man throwing a petrol bomb. The images used were easily recognisable and often featured various aspects of British manhood: the rioter, 'our brave boys' sailing off to the Falklands, and the stroppy striking miners being put in their place by the boys in blue.

The women in these events were often on the sidelines: the wives and girlfriends of the brave boys, waving them off at the docks, and the poor miners' wives who, according to the hype, weren't interested in the politics, but just wanted to go back to 'normal family life'. The one woman who certainly did take centre stage in all this was 'that woman', Margaret Thatcher. The British media took the unusual step of giving sympathetic coverage to a woman who was considered strong and powerful and at the centre of political events.

Before the eighties I'd heard of Margaret Thatcher only because as Education Minister she tried to ban free school milk. At my primary school we had a grudging respect for 'Thatcher the Milk Snatcher' who, we hoped, would save us from the daily ordeal of being forced to drink a third of a pint of warm milk. But the eighties transformed Maggie from 'Thatcher the Milk Snatcher' into a sort of latter-day Churchill. Meanwhile she was ridiculed by much of her Opposition as a bossy wife giving hell to a henpecked nation; politics giving way rapidly to misogyny.

Margaret Thatcher was a whole new excuse for men on the left to stop feeling guilty about sexism. I encountered this attitude again and again – especially when I was involved in the Labour Party Young Socialists in Norwich. Thatcher jokes were so much more acceptable than plain old misogynist ones. And if you didn't laugh you weren't just a humourless feminist, but – horror of horrors – a TORY.

So what were the main events of 'that woman's' decade? Well, the eighties got off to a flying start with 'the riots', which, according to your political perspective, were either a sign of moral decay or the police getting a bloody good hiding. The riots provided endless footage for bloodthirsty news-hounds. They loved this story, which just ran and ran; it had action, conflict and human interest – what more could the public want?

The 1981 riots/uprisings were focused in several large British cities, usually cities with problems of high unemployment and heavy policing. For me the whole period was dominated by a sense of unreality and a questioning of the assumption that 'things like that don't happen here'.

My area of London – Hounslow – became like a ghost town, with an atmosphere you could have cut with a knife. People on the whole were off the streets, glued to TV sets, watching the riots in glorious Technicolor. The news dished out nightly footage of burning barricades and shadowy silhouettes. And the nation was captivated by a combination of voyeurism and horror at the breakdown of law and order.

The greengrocer's where I worked on Saturdays had closed up shop, as had most of the local shops. And walking home from school became very strange. I remember the feeling of the curtains twitching at someone walking down the street, and wanting to get home quickly in case a riot started and I got caught in the middle. I felt as if I was in one of those Westerns when the streets have been cleared for a shoot-out at midday; the calm before the storm. The strangest thing was trying to pretend that everything was normal, in this totally abnormal situation. The streets were empty and the shops were boarded up, yet the boards carried the message 'Business as Usual'. But it certainly wasn't business as usual, and soon the shops found out that there was a whole new meaning to the term 'stock clearance'.

During this time we were sent home early from school 'to avoid trouble', so of course everyone hung around expectantly waiting for the trouble, which never came. The Hounslow Skins were in their element and strutted around the bus garage looking menacing and talking about 'Paki-bashing'. In a way I hoped something would happen just so that these fifteen-year-old Hitlers would get their comeuppance.

Then it all stopped as suddenly as it had started; the boards came down from the shop windows and the news toned down its riots coverage. Now instead of petrol bombs and riot police we saw government ministers visiting burnt-out streets and their residents, secretly thanking God that they didn't live round there.

The next major event to impinge on my consciousness was the Falklands War (or conflict, as the mild-mannered British press liked to call it).

No one I knew took the Falklands seriously at first. Most of the kids I knew were of Irish descent, which made the British army (or navy) a bit of a standing joke in our eyes. There was a spate of people sending out mock call-up cards as a practical joke, but soon it didn't seem so funny any more. I started to regard the Falklands, like the riots, as both frightening and very unreal. Watching the news at this time was like watching old news footage from World War II. The military/political news was combined with an almost show-business-style hype about our heroes going off to fight the 'Hun' (or in this case the 'Argie'). It got to the stage where I almost expected Vera Lynn to pop up on the News at Ten singing 'The White Cliffs of Dover'.

Although in many ways it was totally farcical, the whole fiasco seemed to strike a chord with the nation's young manhood. They were eager to rush off and defend Britain's honour in a place they firmly believed to be somewhere off the coast of Scotland.

The general feeling in Britain at the time was that the whole idea of the task force was a bluff, and that by the time they actually reached the Falklands (wherever they were) the whole thing would be over. However, this was not the case, and it soon became apparent that Britain was to be officially at war with another country. It dawned on people that sending the armed forces was not just an extravagant diplomatic gesture, but an act of war.

By the end of this period even those on the left were supporting the task force for fear of being labelled 'unpatriotic'. Several Labour leaders publicly supported the Falklands War, trying desperately to convince us (and themselves) that British nationalism could be anything other than reactionary.

At first I found it funny that no one in Britain knew where the Falklands were, but as the war continued it became yet another excuse for British racism to show its face. People used to initiate conversations about the Falklands in order to go into some bigoted rant about 'foreigners' generally. At the time people I knew (or half-knew) kept thinking I was Argentinian because I am half-Guyanese (their logic, not mine). Quite often I'd play along with it and pretend to be Argentinian just to annoy them.

Having dealt with 'the foreigners', the British bulldog was now ready to deal with 'the enemy within'. This phenomenon, the internal enemy, had been plaguing the Thatcher government since 1979.

In 1984, the striking miners became the latest challenge of this kind, the latest fly in the red-white-and-blue ointment. The year-long strike was fought on two fronts: the police versus pickets, and the propaganda war. It would seem that the government won the first and the miners the second, with public sympathy on the whole going the miners' way. I remember the weekly food collections in Hounslow High Street being very well supported and a lot of goodwill being shown towards the miners. People did not see them as greedy, or as striking for more money – it was always clear that the issue was pit closures, and the job losses entailed. This struck a chord in Thatcher's Britain, especially after the experience of high and rising unemployment in the early eighties.

The spectre of unemployment and poverty prompted the feeling that Britain was about to return, not to Victorian values, but to the Depression of the thirties. It seemed to me that much of the public sympathy towards the miners was an expression of this anxiety.

Another feature of the early eighties was the changing face of local government. Some very radical local councils emerged at this time, the most infamous being the Labour-controlled Greater London Council, led by the devil incarnate – as the *Daily Mail* would have had us believe – Red Ken Livingstone.

I was living in London while the GLC was in power and it certainly made an impact on me. It was in the news all the time, both nationally and locally, for the 'loony left' policies it pursued. It was really heartening to see politicians taking risks for a change (i.e. sticking to their manifestoes) instead of playing it safe. What distinguished the GLC from the rest of the opposition was that they went completely on the offensive, redefining the agenda of local government politics. They were categorically clear that *all* decisions were political rather than practical or – buzzword of the eighties – 'economic'.

The GLC was attacked both by the government and by the right-wing press for its radical policies. These attacks sometimes took the form of accusations about wasting ratepayers' money but often descended to ridiculing the people and the policies involved. After a five-year battle with the GLC and the other metropolitan councils, the government finally put through legislation to abolish them. But GLC initiatives, such as reducing public transport fares and publicising people's rights to social security, made them popular with Londoners.

Before abolition, the GLC hired advertising billboards around London to put their case across. The posters were eye-catching and straight to the point and you really couldn't miss them, as they were everywhere. The other thing they used to do was to hang a massive banner across County Hall with the unemployment figures printed on it. As County Hall is just across the Thames from the Houses of Parliament, this was a gesture the government just couldn't miss.

As abolition approached, Londoners refused to let the GLC go without a fight, and a high-profile anti-abolition campaign ensued. One of the successes of the campaign was that it did not reduce the issue to a pro- or anti-Ken Livingstone one, but focused on the abolitions of GLC elections and the issue of democracy. Despite its success on a consciousness-raising level the campaign did not manage to stop the abolition, which went through in 1986.

Although there were many problems, the GLC gave many groups in London a chance they would never otherwise have had, and set the rest of the country a dynamic example of municipal socialism.

In the following year, 1987, events in Cleveland brought the issue of child sexual abuse into the public eye. At the time paediatricians in Cleveland were diagnosing an increasing number of children as sexually abused. There were various reactions to this; some more hostile than others.

Police surgeons questioned the validity of the diagnoses, as did local practitioners and the parents of some of the children involved. There was an official inquiry and report, and a great deal of sensationalised media coverage of the 'Cleveland Crisis'.

The implications of Cleveland were far-reaching; it meant that the issue could no longer be swept under the carpet and, more importantly, it challenged the conventional view of child abuse which characterised the problem, simplistically, as one of missing newspaper boys and young girls being accosted by the proverbial 'dirty old man'. Cleveland smashed this myth and revealed a much more complex reality, where it was common for fathers, brothers, uncles, etc., to abuse children – mostly girls – in their own homes.

Furthermore, this was only the tip of the iceberg. If it was this bad in Cleveland, it must mean that nationally hundreds of thousands of children were being abused each year. If this were so, then suddenly the statistics which suggested that one in four girls, and one in ten boys, experienced abuse did not seem so far-fetched after all. But the media and the 'experts' refused to make this connection.

The people who might be expected to deal with such a problem were doing their best to ignore it. The medical profession, social services, the government and the media all turned their backs on the questions raised by Cleveland. They tried to deny not only the implications of the crisis but its very existence.

It was, we were told, all a terrible mistake: the doctors were wrong, the children were wrong, their mothers were wrong. Marietta Higgs, one of the doctors involved, was pilloried by the press, which questioned her professionalism and the diagnostic techniques she used. She was portrayed as a neurotic woman, obsessed with finding sexual abuse where none existed.

On the human-tragedy front, usually a must for the tabloids, we were bombarded with the case histories of 'innocent fathers'. However, the abused children did not have their histories told and were conspicuous by their absence. If you based your impression of the events on the media coverage, you would probably have assumed that not one correct diagnosis had been made.

For all the publicity that surrounded the events in Cleveland, very little real public discussion of child abuse occurred. Cleveland could have provided the perfect opportunity for the issue to be aired publicly and for some progress to be made. Instead we saw a vicious backlash against those who dragged the skeleton out of the cupboard. This involved an extraordinary alliance between the police, courts, the medical profession, the media and political activists from both left and right. It was amazing to watch the alacrity with which various groups on the British left allied themselves with 'the Establishment' in order to resist a feminist analysis of child sexual abuse.

Looking back on it a few years later, the whole thing seems like a storm in a teacup. Nothing seems to have moved on. Cleveland didn't lead the way to a greater understanding of child abuse, or secure a more broad-based commitment to fighting it.

Things looked bad as we neared the end of the decade: with the GLC abolished, the miners defeated, and the unemployed on their bikes. Thatcherism swept through the country like an avenging angel and few were spared. So who's next in the firing line? Feminists campaigning against pornography? British Muslims? Anyone who knows anyone who might have AIDS? Bigotry seemed to be gaining an acceptable face, and was increasingly enshrined in the law.

On the parliamentary side, the Alton Bill and Clause 28 of the Local Government Bill were introduced. Two strong campaigns emerged to fight these Bills. The Alton Bill was yet another attempt to restrict abortion; it was proposed by David Alton, the latest in a long line of MPs to go on a 'moral crusade' on this issue.

The Alton Bill aimed to lower the time limit on abortion, and the Fight the Alton Bill (FAB) campaign was set up to oppose it. FAB was successful in its immediate aim of fighting this particular Bill and also in furthering the debate on abortion. It opened up wider discussion about women's control over their own bodies and fertility, and consistently defined itself as pro-choice – which put Alton and his supporters in the position of being 'anti-choice'. The campaign also emphasised abortion as a *political* issue and linked late abortions with, for example, NHS cuts, instead of arguing for time limits simply in terms of the law.

David Alton actually came to address a meeting of his supporters in Norwich, while the Bill was going through Parliament. In the local FAB group we decided to picket the meeting, but it didn't go quite as planned. It turned into a bit of a farce, with various people from FAB running around trying to find the meeting in order to picket it. When we eventually did find it, the Alton supporters were more than willing to eject us from their public meeting, but despite a few scuffles with the Militant Christians, the action was successful and the meeting was cancelled. Soon after this we heard the good news that the Alton Bill had *not* become law.

All this took me back to the heady days of 'Fight the Corrie Bill'. I was still at school at the time, and still a Catholic, when I went on a demonstration against the Corrie Bill in 1979, with my mum and sister. Unfortunately there was a counter-demonstration by various anti-abortion groups and, even more unfortunately, some people from our church were there – on the counter-demo. Imagine my horror at being spotted by half the congregation of St Bridget's and Our Lady of Sorrows at an abortion march. They were none too pleased when they realised that we were on 'the other side'.

As the Alton Bill was laid to rest, the campaign against Clause 28 was just gaining momentum. Clause 28 sought to ban 'the promotion of homosexuality' by local authorities. It was regarded by many people in the Stop the Clause campaign as a backlash against various lesbian and gay projects which had been set up during the '80s, often funded by the more radical local councils.

'Stop the Clause' was a campaign which handled its own publicity very well. Clause 28 demonstrations were not just the usual dreary marches through the rain (though there were a few of those!). Instead there was a spate of actions with lesbians leaping out of pink closets, abseiling into the House of Lords and hijacking the News at Six.

Such creative political tactics did wonders for the morale of people involved in the campaign. I was involved in Norwich Stop the Clause and it was a real boost for us every time someone got publicity for the campaign by doing something even more outrageous. The Clause, as they say, put the 'camp' back into 'campaign'!

The campaign did not succeed in 'Stopping the Clause', but I would say that in terms of mobilising people, publicity, etc., it was successful in a number of other ways. There were many people on marches and demonstrations then who had never been politically active before.

As a way forward for the 1990s I would like to see people getting involved in politics (in whatever form) because they believe things *can* change, rather than from a sense of duty, or worse still as a kind of hobby.

I think the '80s have been a hard ten years in many ways, but the fact that as feminists as socialists we are still going is an achievement in itself. We may look back at the 1960s and 1970s and yearn for the days when 'everyone was radical' – but how much of that radicalism was superficial? Instead of lamenting the '80s as a period when 'the movement died' and all the activists became cynics, we should see it as a sort of weeding-out process. Those who are still in there are there for the duration, and we are stronger for knowing who our real allies are.

16

Strategies and Visions for a Women's Movement

Spare Rib Collective

The last ten years have been difficult ones for the women's movement, as for all progressive movements. Right-wing forces have exerted a devastating power worldwide. In Britain, during these years of increased repression, we have witnessed a serious fragmentation and a lack of strategy within the Women's Movement, which have not made our plight any easier.

Being on the Spare Rib Collective during this time has been an extremely challenging, and at times a painful experience. It has also been an empowering one, and a process which has changed the way we view ourselves and the Women's Movement.

Despite the difficulties of the '80s we feel there has been an increased awareness of the huge potential of an international Women's Movement to effect change on the current global situation. Here, we look at some of the reasons why we feel the Women's Movement has the potential to challenge the powers that be, and some of the reasons why this potential is not being fully realised.

Before we came to Spare Rib we all saw the Women's Movement and *Spare Rib* magazine as something quite removed from ourselves and our realities. We associated the Women's Movement with white middle-class women, whose world-view was very different from our own.

One member of the Collective put it this way during our discussions for this piece:

The word feminist never really came into my vocabulary – except as a derogatory term. I'd seen *Spare Rib*, but as a Black woman I had no contact with it or it with me.

None the less, via different routes, we arrived at Spare Rib, and in wandering into this setting, we started to realise that this movement did and must relate to us. There were things the Women's Movement seemed to offer that no other contemporary movements could offer us.

We began to see that our exclusion had been perpetuated by a small minority of women, who had hijacked the Women's Movement, defining it narrowly in line with their own interests and privilege, and depleting it of any meaning for the vast majority of women on this planet.

The term 'feminism' has come to denote an elitist and exclusionary movement – something which at times feels like an old girls' network. This has alienated a huge majority of women from participating: women whose energy, intellect and creativity would be a major contribution to this movement and its efforts to create change.

This kind of exclusion is tragic. A member of the Collective described her experience:

I came to Spare Rib to do some part-time work, and I started to realise a potential. Despite the exclusionary way things were dealt with, the issues that were being dealt with did in fact relate to me. There is a great sadness in me that something so much a part of me could have been kept from me.

In an interview with *Spare Rib*, Bernice Johnson Reagon, of *Sweet Honey in the Rock*, describes her experience:

As Black women . . . we had to negotiate space for ourselves. The spaces generally were never big enough to support us – but we noticed the spaces tended not to be big enough to support women who were aligned with men, women who saw themselves as being part of a people which included men and children. We were in a radical movement which was too small for most of our radicals.[1]

For us, this exclusion is one of the most serious failures of the Women's Movement, and has been instrumental in preventing us from realising our full potential as an international movement. This exclusion has occurred in three major ways – on the basis of race, class, and as a result of the colonial relationship which typifies so many relations between the European Liberation movements and Liberation movements in the so-called 'Third World'. Sadly, this mimicking of established patterns of classism, racism, and imperialism by many who openly declare their revulsion for these relations has halted our possible principled unity as women and sisters, and hence our progress as a revolutionary movement with the ability to find a new way of relating as women, as women and men, across cultures, and among nations.

In trying to understand the potential of the Women's Movement, we need to ask: *What is the Women's Movement?*

For many, the term Women's Movement has become synonymous with the European Women's Movement and 'feminism'. For us, when we talk about the Women's Movement, we are not referring to the European Women's Movement, although that is clearly a part of the Women's Movement. We are not referring only to the last decades. We are talking about a movement and a tradition which predate the modern

Women's Movement – a tradition of leadership and struggle maintained by women worldwide, which goes back a long way and has existed across race and class. It is out of this tradition that the modern-day Women's Movement has evolved.

In trying to understand what the modern-day Women's Movement is, there is no specific theoretical work to turn to, and no central organising committee to contact for a definitive blueprint.

Some may see this as a setback, leading to a necessary fragmentation and inability for collective action. For us, this is one of the most potentially dynamic and exciting aspects of the Women's Movement, affording it a flexibility and a potential for a unity with diversity that are liberating in themselves, especially when compared to other political movements this century.

Despite the lack of a definitive theoretical viewpoint, we believe that at its core the Women's Movement has an unshakeable ethos – an ethos which we believe has the potential to develop a new political vision, with alternative frameworks and strategies.

The lack of a definitive theoretical viewpoint has had positive effects. It has de-emphasised theory and dogma and rules, textbook politics – something which has dogged many a political movement these past decades – and this has led to an emphasis on 'process' and 'practice'.

This emphasis on process has led to a recognition of what *exists*, which determines to a certain extent our methods and practice, and what might be relevant political action. It is out of this process that an ethos emerges – spoken or unspoken.

What *does exist* is women, who have come together, forming organisations across the globe, to fight the widest diversity of oppressions. This, by its very existence, creates certain understandings and visions.

For example, an international movement necessitates a

sincere respect for diversity. This respect is about hearing each other, engaging with and understanding each other's dignity and urgency. It is not about exclusion.

A true respect for diversity entails the breaking down of hierarchies and competition, and an end to the endless power struggle. Put into practice, by a global political movement which constitutes half of the world's population, this ethos presents a serious threat.

In their book *Development Crises and Alternative Visions: Third World Women's Perspectives*, Gita Sen and Caren Grown explain it this way:

Beneath this diversity, feminism has as its unshakeable core a commitment to breaking down the structures of gender subordination, and a vision for women as full and equal participants with men at all levels of societal life. There has been considerable confusion and misunderstanding among women around this question. The recognition of the existence of gender subordination and the need to break down its structures has often led to the wrong conclusions – that it engenders monolithic and universal issues, strategies and methods, applicable to all women in all societies at all times. But a political movement that is potentially global in scope needs greater flexibility, openness, and sensitivity to issues and methods as defined by different groups of women for themselves.[2]

Issues and methods – as defined by different groups of women for themselves – are for us an integral part of a global political movement, especially at this time in history. It is about the politics of self-determination. Self-definition and self-determination are about women speaking for themselves, defining our own oppression, and setting the agenda for our liberation struggle. It entails respect for difference, and the will actively to reject and break down the inevitable hierarchy and power structures which develop when one group of women speaks for another.

When others speak for you, they most often get it wrong, and this adds to our oppression – especially when that other who is speaking for you is from a group which has oppressed you for centuries.

All our histories shape who we all are today. Those women who come from groups which have a long history of enforcing a hierarchy based on race and class may feel that somehow control and power and agenda-setting are their domain but they are not. Part of preserving that domain and maintaining their power and control is to speak for all other women. This is about maintaining hierarchies, not breaking them down. It is a form of imperialism and elitism which needs to be opposed.

In a letter to *Spare Rib*, Cecily, a Black woman and Chris, a white working-class woman, describing their experiences at the 5th Conference of European Socialist Feminists, explain the way in which this hierarchy is maintained:

Ruling and middle-class white feminists have always had power to silence Black and white women by marginalising and isolating them. They say that our arguments are 'good' but don't take up the issues raised by them. They keep women short of the information they need to be part of the decision-making process, and they set the agendas. We write letters and they ignore them.[3]

This outmoded notion of hierarchy, and negation of each other's realities and oppressions, is deeply offensive. It is maintaining what has been, and continues to be, a criminal set of power relations which we need to be rid of, in order to develop a new political framework with which we can move ahead.

In finding a new political framework, we do not want to fall into a trap of engaging in a deadlocked battle over which is the 'true feminism', or what are truly 'women's issues'.

We believe that by definition the Women's Movement must incorporate, as part of its struggle, all the oppressions which affect women worldwide. This means embracing a broad range of issues.

For us, *everything is linked*. We do not believe that it is possible to separate the oppression of gender subordination from other oppressions. For a majority of women worldwide, other oppressions – of race, class, capitalism and imperialism – are intricately interconnected with their subordination as women, and their liberation. Furthermore, the subordination of women for centuries has been about our exclusion from shaping the major issues of our times. These are critical times. They require our vigilant attention as a women's movement. Our solutions are sorely needed.

Gita Sen and Caren Grown put it like this:

Over the past twenty years, the Women's Movement has debated the links between the eradication of gender subordination and of other forms of social and economic oppression based on nation, class, or ethnicity. We strongly support the position in this debate, that feminism cannot be monolithic in its issues, goals, and strategies, since it constitutes the political expression of the concerns and interests of women from different regions, classes, nationalities, and ethnic backgrounds. While gender subordination has universal elements, feminism cannot be based on a rigid concept of universality that negates the wide variation in women's experience. There is, and must be a diversity of feminisms, responsive to the different needs and concerns of different women, and defined by them for themselves.

For us there is no one enemy, or root cause from which all else spins. We see it more as a web of oppressions, feeding off each other. Patriarchy is a main component of this web, and one part of the web, which as women only we can expose and challenge. We can also use our understanding of this power imbalance, and how it affects us, to understand other power imbalances with which it joins forces. The power imbalance among women and men, among races, classes, and nations, have interacted to cause a nightmarish world for most of the people on this planet. Our attack is aimed at all those who are responsible for maintaining the systems that in turn maintain and perpetuate these power imbalances.

Eradicating women's oppression means making a new world for all humankind. Gita Sen and Caren Grown sum up our feelings:

. . . we strongly affirm that feminism strives for the broadest and deepest development of society and human beings, free of all systems of domination . . . In this context, we believe that it is from the perspective of the most oppressed – that is, women who suffer on account of class, race, and nationality – that we can most clearly grasp the nature of the links in the chain of oppression, and explore the kinds of actions that we must now take.

Notes

1. *Sweet Honey: Passing As Musicians* – interview with Bernice Johnson Reagon, *Spare Rib*, no. 206, October 1989.
2. *Development, Crises and Alternative Visions, Third World Women's Perspectives*, Gita Sen and Caren Grown for Development Alternatives with Women for a New Era (DAWN), Earthscan Publications, London, 1988.
3. *'Have You Read My Latest Article?'* – *5th Conference Of European Socialist Feminists*, letter to *Spare Rib* from Cecily and Chris, *Spare Rib*, no. 209, February 1990.

Notes on Contributors

Norah Al-Ani

I was born in 1970 in Kirkuk, Iraq, of an Irish mother and an Arabic father. In 1980 I came with my mother and sisters to England, where I have been living since. I now work in a Women's Centre with which I have been involved for many years.

Alison Bark

I was born in Warrington on 1 August 1965, and suffered brain damage soon after birth. I was educated at ordinary primary schools, a day school for disabled children, and the Sixth Form Department of a 'normal' comprehensive school. I am currently studying for an Open University degree and living at home with my parents.

Louise Donald

I was born in Wishaw, Strathclyde, in 1961. I studied English and Philosophy at York University from 1978 to 1981 and subsequently worked in the theatre until 1989, when I started work as an administrator at a dance school in London. I also got involved with the Campaign Against Pornography at this time, and found myself thrown in at the deep end by agreeing to participate in TV and radio debates on this issue. I'm seriously thinking about going back to Scotland (perhaps in time to canvass for the SNP before the next general election?).

Jayne Kelly

I live in the country with my lover and our two children. I'm committed to total disarmament and believe in non-violent direct action to achieve this. I'm a painter and an organic gardener.

Jacqueline McCafferty

I was born in Derry City in 1964; I lived with my mother and brother in the Bogside until I was eleven years old. I studied Psychology and Sociology at Sunderland Polytechnic, and before going to college travelled in Europe; later I travelled to North and Central America, and then Asia and the Far East. I returned to Derry in 1989 and am currently working as an unemployment researcher in the Bogside, one of the most deprived areas of Derry. Politically I would describe myself as a moderate socialist, nationalist and feminist.

Ruth McManus

In Glasgow, on the dole – looking to change the world, get research funding, and have a good time.

Valerie Malcolm

I am twenty years old, a young Black woman. I am now studying Applied Social Sciences with Social Work at Bradford University. It's a four-year course, and I am in my third year. I have an autoimmune disease called SLE (Systemic Lupus Erythmatosus). I have written about this and about my experiences of the health service in Britain today.

Sharmila Mukerji

I was born in 1968 in Solihull, West Midlands. My father is Indian, my mother English; and I am the second eldest of four children. I was educated at King Edward VI High School for Girls, Birmingham (1979–86). I applied to study medicine, but accepted a place at London Contemporary Dance School instead. At present I am in the final year of a BA (Hons) course in Contemporary Dance. On completion of the course I wish to perform, teach, and travel. I am also involved in the LCDS Student Union, and a member of Amnesty International and the Nicaragua Solidarity Campaign.

Mandy Nichol

I was born in March 1963, and lived most of my life in a small market town in Galloway, Scotland. I have recently left both town and my marriage to begin a new life of independence with my son (aged three and a half). I also hope to continue my studies with the Open University, in the hope that someday I will get a degree. In the meantime I would like to become more aware of feminist issues and become more actively involved in the struggle.

Chris Pegg

I was born in Derby in 1962 and moved in 1985 to Brighton, 'the lesbian capital of the South', where I have worked hard, learnt a lot, and now feel myself to be part of the 'community'. I'm a lesbian, a single mother, and Sagittarius with Scorpio rising. I share my life with two other women, an eleven year old, a cat, a hamster and two goldfish. I am currently in my second year of a part-time MA in Women's Studies at Kent University, and trying to decide in which direction I should move next.

Agnes Quashie

I was born of Carriacouan parents who, after living in Trinidad for many years, came to the UK, where I was born in 1965. I have studied at the University of Essex for the last four years, and I am currently completing my MA in the Sociology of Literature. The area on which I am concentrating for my dissertation is Afro-Caribbean Literature and Western Discourse/Theory, an area in which I am greatly interested, but one that I have not as yet fully developed. Someday I hope to go on to lecture on this topic and related areas, but there still remain several hurdles that I must cross in order to get there.

Clare Ramsaran

I am of Indo-Guyanese and Irish descent, and was born and brought up in London. I recently finished a degree in Development Studies in Norwich and I'm now pleased to be out of full-time education. My interest in writing started when I spent a hectic year working at *Outwrite* women's newspaper. This is an experience I would not have missed for the world, and like many others I felt the loss when *Outwrite* had to fold through lack of funding. I eventually hope to be a journalist.

Mary Smeeth

I was born in London in 1962, but we moved north when I was three and I grew up largely in Hull. I have two brothers. At eighteen I went to Bristol and ended up working as a copywriter in an advertising agency. In 1985 I went to the University of East Anglia (UEA) to do a degree in English. I was lucky enough to be there when Su Kappeler was teaching; she had put feminist politics on to the agenda and made it possible to see how a feminist theory and a feminist practice were inseparable. I was involved in several campaigns in the late eighties, including Stop the Clause and FAB, and I am currently a member of WAIST (Women Against International Sex Trafficking). I am now back in Norwich after a year in Manchester, and researching into the writing of Elizabeth Robins (1862–1952), who was a feminist and militant campaigner for women's suffrage. I believe that the neglect of the work of a woman who has made such a significant contribution to the development of feminist ideas is a major loss to many areas of contemporary feminist debate. It is my ambition to see her work back in print in the 1990s.

Spare Rib Collective

The current Spare Rib Collective members are Esther Bailey, Marcel Farry, Elorine Grant, Jennifer Mourin and Sarah Payton.

The magazine was started in 1972, by a group of women who were dissatisfied with their marginalised role in the underground press at the time. Their aim was to produce a popular, accessible publication which would 'put Women's Liberation on the news stands'.

Eighteen years later, Spare Rib is still here to tell a tale or two. Owned by no one, Spare Rib has been taken care of by numerous collectives over the years, with varying visions of the women's movement. It has a life of its own, and an incredible will to live. Long may it live.

Emma Wallis

I was born in Sheffield in 1965. I left school in 1982 to join the dole queue, and remained a government statistic until 1987. I was involved with Sheffield Women Against Pit Closures during the 1984–5 miners' strike. I am currently at Northern College, and hoping to make my mother proud by going to university in October 1990.

WIGAN PIER REVISITED
Poverty and Politics in the 80s
Beatrix Campbell

A brilliant exposé of poverty and politics in Britain today

In 1937 George Orwell published *The Road to Wigan Pier*, an account of his famous 'urban ride' among the people and places of the Great Depression. Fifty years later we are living through a second Great Depression, and this time the journey north has been made by a woman – like Orwell a journalist and a socialist, but, unlike him, working class and a feminist.

Wigan Pier Revisited is a devastating record of what Beatrix Campbell saw and heard in towns and cities ravaged by poverty and unemployment. She talks to young mothers on the dole, to miners and their families, to school leavers, battered wives, factory workers, redundant workers, discovers what work, home, family, politics and dignity mean for working-class people today. Out of this comes her passionate plea for genuine socialism, one informed by feminism, drawing its strength from the grass roots and responding to people's real needs.

TRUTH, DARE OR PROMISE
Girls Growing Up in the Fifties
Edited by Liz Heron

'An absorbing, meticulous, beautifully written anthology of richly various remembered girlhoods in the optimistic days of the early Welfare State. In its pleasurable way an important piece of social history. I read with delight and recognition' – *Angela Carter*

In this superb collection of autobiographical writing, twelve women who grew into feminism in the 1970s look back on their childhoods. Some grew up in homes of pinching poverty, others in an orderliness so unbending as to be drab, still others in an easy security. In feeling, circumstance, class and culture, their experiences were as diverse as they were keenly felt. But the common feature of this post-war Britain of 'you never had it so good' were the two great landmarks of the Welfare State and the Education Act. It gave to many of these girlhoods, so like and yet so unlike those of their mothers, a sense of possibility, of aspiration to a different future. These are intimate, personal memoirs, ordinary and impossible stories that remind us how individual lives are shaped in infinitely complex ways.